Nolan, Jeannette Covert.
Shot heard round the world.

DATE DUE

4-30-84			
12-9-92			
DE 11 '96			

THE SHOT HEARD ROUND THE WORLD

The Story of Lexington and Concord

On April 19, 1775, a group of colonists hurriedly gathered at Lexington, Massachusetts, to block a detachment of British soldiers on their way to Concord where American arms were stored. Suddenly a shot was fired—by whom no one knows —and before the fateful day was over the American Revolution had begun. Treating both the British and American points of view with complete honesty and understanding, this book dramatically brings to life the great men and events which culminated in one of the most decisive days in this nation's history.

"By the rude bridge that arched the flood,
Their flag to April's breeze unfurled,
Here once the embattled farmers stood,
And fired the shot heard round the world. . . ."

RALPH WALDO EMERSON

THE SHOT HEARD ROUND THE WORLD

The Story of Lexington and Concord

●●●●●●

by Jeannette Covert Nolan

Maps by Barry Martin

JULIAN MESSNER
New York

Published simultaneously in the United States and Canada by
Julian Messner, a division of Simon & Schuster, Inc.
1 West 39 Street, New York, N.Y. 10018. All rights reserved.

Ninth Printing, 1972

Printed in the United States of America

ISBN 0-671-32605-8 MCE

Library of Congress Catalog Card No. 63-8652

Contents

". . . A history of the first war of the United States is a very different thing from a history of the American Revolution. . . . The revolution was in the minds of the people and in the union of the colonies, both of which were accomplished before hostilities commenced. This revolution and union were gradually forming from the years 1760 to 1776."

JOHN ADAMS

". . . They have begun it—that either party can do; and we will end it—that only one can do."

JOSEPH WARREN
April 19, 1775

The English colonies existing in America at the time of the engagements at Lexington and Concord, participating actively thereafter in the War of the Revolution, and in 1776, with the Declaration of Independence, combining to form the United States of America, were:

New Hampshire	Delaware
Massachusetts	Maryland
Connecticut	Virginia
Rhode Island	Georgia
New York	North Carolina
New Jersey	South Carolina
Pennsylvania	

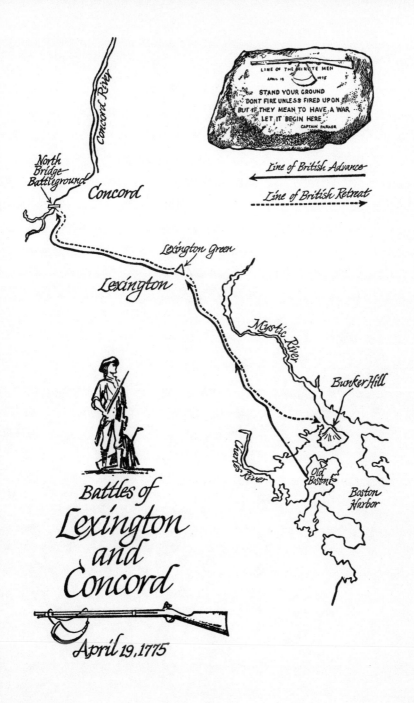

LINE OF THE MINUTE MEN
APRIL 19   1775

STAND YOUR GROUND
DONT FIRE UNLESS FIRED UPON
BUT IF THEY MEAN TO HAVE A WAR
LET IT BEGIN HERE

CAPTAIN PARKER

Line of British Advance

Line of British Retreat

Concord River

North
Bridge
Battleground

Concord

Lexington Green

Lexington

Mystic River

Bunker Hill

Charles River

Old
Boston

Boston
Harbor

Battles of
Lexington
and
Concord

April 19, 1775

1

●●●●●●

Dawn

John Parker scrutinized the men drawn up in two thin lines on Lexington green.

"Stand fast," he said. "Stand fast. They're bound for Concord, we're told. Let them pass and don't molest them, without they begin it first."

Parker spoke quietly, but firmly. Middle-aged, erect and stalwart, he was the captain of the Lexington militia and well aware of the responsibility resting now on his broad shoulders.

The date was April 19, 1775, a Wednesday morning, very early, just five o'clock. The sun, rising clear and round, cast slanted saffron rays over the green's grassy triangle and the buildings sparsely bordering it: several large frame houses painted white, Buckman's Tavern, a shed, a stable and the blacksmith's shop. Inside the triangle, on the edge that faced the road to Concord, were the village school, the church, the square belfry with its peaked roof—and the men, poised stiffly at attention.

Parker counted them: the Lexington militia, the "minutemen," so called for the oath they had sworn, to respond in a minute to any emergency. He counted to seventy, and stopped—seventy in all, some scarcely more than stripling youths, some gray-bearded oldsters, one-third of the lot John Parker's kith and kin by either blood or marriage, and every one his friend and neighbor.

He thought they trusted him and would obey him.

They were not in uniform, for they possessed no uniforms, but wore workaday clothes, rough shirts open at the throat, jackets and breeches of homespun, yarn stockings and stout shoes—haphazard garments, whatever they had been able to find at hand and scramble into when roused from their warm beds at midnight by the clattering hoofs in the street, the rap of knuckles on door panels, the express rider's cry running from house to house:

"The British are coming! The British—"

Snatching up flintlocks, they had rushed forth to the green, the place appointed for rendezvous if danger threatened. And thereafter, for a while, excitement and confusion had gripped them.

Fortunately, Captain Parker kept his head. "Those of you who are furnished, load your guns," he said. "Those lacking ammunition, get it from the magazine in the meetinghouse and rejoin the company."

So they had assembled—and waited, taut and anxious. The moon shone ghostly pale in the sky above them, the wind sharpened and blew chill, the slow hours ticked by. The men shivered, fidgeted, muttered one to another.

The express rider from Boston, had it been Revere? Yes, Paul Revere. Ah, a thorough patriot, an official courier for the Boston Sons of Liberty! But what he said, was it true? Could it be true? Were British regulars, a thousand strong, really marching to seize the cannon, the powder and ball, the tents and kettles and medicines—the precious supplies accumulated with such effort, bit by bit, and hoarded at Concord?

Or was this a false alarm?

The waiting was difficult, grueling. Only Captain Parker remainded calm. He sent four scouts separately back toward Boston, seeking news, later reports. The scouts seemed to vanish into the night, darkness enveloped and swallowed them. Were they trapped, captured?

The hours ticked on, as if forever. At four o'clock, with dawn streaking the eastern horizon—and no further word, nothing—Parker had dismissed the company.

"The alarm was false," he said. "It must have been."

Singly or in groups, the men drifted from the green, some going to their homes and frightened families, but most of them following the captain to Buckman's, where in the tavern taproom they consulted, sipped mugs of steaming rum punch and, vaguely uneasy, waited still.

Then one of the scouts, Thaddeus Brown, reappeared suddenly, his horse at the gallop.

Parker strode from the tavern. "Brown! What is it?"

Brown gasped his reply. The redcoats were coming, all right! They were just around the bend in the road, soon they would be in plain sight!

Parker nodded grimly. "Ring the bell," he said. "Discharge a warning volley. William Diamond, beat your drum."

Hastily the bell was rung, a volley of shots discharged. William Diamond, an eager lad of eighteen, smartly rattled his drumsticks.

The lines formed again.

And now here they were: the seventy minutemen of Lexington, ready and resolute, eyes fixed on their captain. It was five o'clock, and the ground beneath their feet vibrated faintly to the measured tread of an approaching regiment.

"Stand fast," Parker said. "Remember, our sole duty is to protect our women and children, the town. Don't fire unless fired upon. This is not war. There is no war in America—as yet."

Was that all he said?

Sergeant William Munroe, standing near him, thought the captain added something, a stern sentence:

"But if they mean to have a war, let it begin here."

Sergeant Munroe would always believe and avow that Captain Parker added that sentence.

No, there was as yet no war. Certainly not! This was merely an excursion, peaceable in nature, and planned to be secretly executed. But Lieutenant Colonel Francis Smith was convinced that somehow the secret had leaked out.

Colonel Smith commanded the twenty-one companies of British grenadiers and light infantry dispatched from Boston. Increasingly during the night, on the journey of eleven or twelve miles (to him it seemed twice that long!), he had become conscious of a strangeness prevailing everywhere, undercurrents stirring, mysterious rustlings behind farmyard fences, the occasional detonation of a distant gun, a lamp flaring in a cottage window, furtive shadows shifting in the woods. He was amply provided with spies; his spies were spread through the whole area. He suspected that the countryfolk must also have spies in plenty—busy rascals!

Colonel Smith was somewhat elderly, very fat, deliberate in habit—and tired. The horse he rode had a lumbering gait, his saddle was lumpy and uncomfortable. And though not unduly keen-witted or sensitive, he had apprehensions about this venture, this excursion, especially if the purpose had been discovered, as he felt sure it had. Oh, he would see the job through (and, of course, successfully) but he didn't fancy it; he wished that General Gage hadn't chosen him to conduct it.

General Thomas Gage was the King's military governor of

Massachusetts and commander-in-chief of all the British
soldiers stationed in America, five thousand of them in Boston. On Tuesday evening, Gage had summoned Colonel
Smith and instructed him.

Colonel Smith was to proceed to Concord, passing through
Lexington en route. At Concord he was to confiscate and
destroy the assorted supplies stored, and probably concealed,
there. The greater portion of the supplies, Gage said, had
been stolen from the British magazines in Boston, smuggled
out piecemeal over a period of months. He gave Colonel
Smith a map of Concord; penstrokes on the map indicated
houses and barns in which the stolen goods were most likely
to be hidden. The move to reclaim them was to be made
discreetly, in a manner that would not provoke attack. No
resort to weapons unless resistance was shown!

"You will take care," Gage advised, "that the soldiers do
not plunder the inhabitants or hurt private property."

Colonel Smith had received the order without question,
respectfully. All of Gage's officers respected their chief, but
some important personages in civilian circles, both here and
at home in England, were not so impressed with him: Lord
Dartmouth, the King's colonial secretary, for example.

It was known that Lord Dartmouth criticized Thomas
Gage as being too lenient with the Americans he governed.
Lord Dartmouth said the King was angry, dissatisfied with
Gage's patience and tolerance. These people (these "patri-
ots," as they now quaintly described themselves!) were the
King's subjects. How dared they disregard his laws, refuse to
pay the taxes—the moderate taxes—which the Crown law-
fully asked of them?

Lord Dartmouth advocated a firmer policy, stricter rules,
severe punishment for offenders. Take the "patriot" leaders
into custody! he urged. A recent letter notified General Gage
that other members of the King's cabinet and a majority in

the Parliament agreed with Lord Dartmouth. Parliament declared Massachusetts to be in a "state of rebellion," from which it must be redeemed—if necessary, by coercion.

So it looked (didn't it?) as if the higher-ups were pushing Gage into a situation where he was obliged to act, to *do* something. And one result was his decision to send a party by night to Concord.

Perhaps Gage had erred in judgment. The thought of that went with Colonel Smith, nagging at him, as he jogged along the dark road, very tired and rather short of breath.

Well, nobody but a fool would deny that relations between England and her American colonists, deteriorating steadily for many years, were now crumbling at an incredible rate, "incidents" marked by violence often occurring. Yes, and however bad things might be elsewhere, in Massachusetts they were always worse, much worse, the incidents more frequent, the violence more marked—with Boston the very storm center!

Rebellion? Colonel Smith smiled wryly. Lord Dartmouth, the cabinet and Parliament members, sitting safe and snug in London, had put the case mildly. "*I* should have said *chaos*," grumbled Colonel Smith.

And how on earth could such a move as this one be made secretly and with discretion if the countryside was alerted?

Worried, thinking his sober thoughts, watching the moon fade and sink, the sun rising, Colonel Smith heard abruptly the clang of a church bell, a burst of musketry, drumbeats.

"The militia at Lexington," he said to himself. "They're expecting us. Will they show resistance?"

He sighed and hoped not!

Major John Pitcairn had the advance columns, six companies of light infantry, four hundred men. The grenadiers, under Colonel Smith, were slightly to the rear.

Major Pitcairn was an efficient and experienced officer of the Royal Marines. His present assignment with the infantry was only temporary—and not entirely to his liking.

The trouble was that he doubted the temper of his troops. Most of them were seasoned veterans who had fought with courage on famous battlefields in Europe. They were, really, the flower of Gage's army, and they knew it. They had their traditions and reputation, their pride. In normal circumstances, their behavior could be predicted and relied upon; but they felt now that they were being ill-used.

Major Pitcairn was inclined to believe some reason existed for the feeling. Mustered out of billets at ten o'clock Tuesday night; hurried across Boston Common to the shore of the Back Bay, with no idea of their destination, the captains constantly cautioning silence ("Hush! Hush!"); ferried across the bay to Cambridge; disembarked in a swamp where they waded and stumbled about in shallow water, slime and weeds up to their knees; delayed there until two o'clock, while horses were obtained for the officers and packets of food distributed (rations which were promptly discarded, for who wanted the extra burden?); marched then on a rutted, unfamiliar road; delayed again to allow Colonel Smith to confer with the officers; marched again, with their fine boots sopping wet, their white leggings, the tails of their beautiful scarlet coats mud-stained and dripping—

What kind of treatment was this for elite soldiers? Little wonder they were puzzled, resentful, murmuring irritably, cursing their luck, cursing Francis Smith as an ancient, blundering fuss-budget.

In Major Pitcairn's opinion, there would have been no harm in telling them where they were going, and why. The mission should have been explained, he thought.

"Control them," Smith had said. "Don't let the reins slip. Do nothing that might provoke attack."

Major Pitcairn had repeated the order to his captains; it sifted down through the ranks: "Don't fire unless fired on."

Would the men bear it in mind? They must! It was essential that they bear it in mind.

But suppose they were challenged at some village, some fence corner along the way? All through the tedious night the possibility haunted Major Pitcairn. Now in the flush of dawn, it pricked his thoughts like a thistle. Guns had boomed briefly just beyond the next bend in the road. Were they to be challenged in Lexington. And if so, what then?

Major Pitcairn had observed these troopers, these proud, elite, splendidly outfitted veterans. He knew them pretty well. They hated the straggling, ragtag provincials who were loosely organized in the colonial militia. They felt for them the withering scorn of the trained professional for the awkward, ignorant amateur. Minutemen? Farmers, they were, yokels, a bunch of louts! And more than that—liars, traitors! By law and by rights, the colonial militia companies were pledged to serve the King, the interests of the Crown. But the pledge had been forgotten. Now, in their poor fashion, they served a different master, the "cause of freedom," a fantastic something that drove them to parade and drill at times of their own selection, to make outlandish public demonstrations—to harass, taunt and mock their betters!

In fact, the British regulars hated any and all Americans who could be classified as patriots. And why not? they argued. Ever since their arrival in Boston they had suffered the patriots' sneers and insults. They would have retaliated, of course, if permitted to; they yearned to retaliate. But General Gage restrained them.

The regulars had a nickname for Gage; it was the Old Woman. Sometimes, though seldom, they managed to get in a few sly digs, a knock or two, a blow with a clenched fist— when the Old Woman wasn't looking. They cherished the

dream that a day would come when the score could be
evened.

Major Pitcairn was determined that this should not be the
day.

Where the road straightened, the view was unobstructed.
Pitcairn raised his telescope, squinted through it. He could
see the Lexington green, the double line of militiamen.
Fringing the triangle were spectators, curious townsfolk pre-
sumably, perhaps a hundred of them, including some women
and children. From the windows of the tavern and the big
white houses, people gaped and peered. On the doorstep of
one house a woman held a baby balanced on her hip, while
a brood of little tots clung to her skirts.

Pitcairn lowered his glass. He was not surprised that the
militia company was there, not at all; he had known it would
be. But that the assemblage should be so small surprised him
—so small and so oddly quiet. They were motionless: the
men, their captain, the drummer and a fifer, like figures in a
picture or statues carved in stone.

What was their intention? To block the progress of the
British? Or to let them pass, then trail after them, taking pot-
shots from ambush?

Well, they were armed; therefore, they must be dealt with.
Surround and disarm, that was the thing. The task would be
swift and simple.

Pitcairn issued terse orders. "Prime and load. Advance
slowly, keeping your ranks—and don't fire."

He gestured two of his captains forward and rode on to
the green.

John Parker stared at the advancing force. It choked the
narrow road and seemed to stretch back interminably into
the distance: a corps of drummers, sergeants carrying regi-
mental banners and the flag of England, a sea of tall arched

helmets and gleaming bayoneted guns. Paul Revere, the messenger from Boston, had estimated them as a thousand strong. Parker would have set the number higher.

Riding in front came a handsome major in the uniform of the Royal Marines, escorted by a pair of British captains. They wore white wigs under their plumed black bonnets, gold buttons and crossed sashes on their waistcoats, Spanish pistols and swords in scabbards at their belts. Parker identified the marine officer as Major Pitcairn, of whom Paul Revere had spoken knowingly. He thought Pitcairn looked solemn; the two captains, nameless to him, were smiling insolently.

What would they say—and do?

They came on closer, very close, and when a tossed pebble could have touched them, they halted.

Pitcairn drew his sword with a flourish. "Lay down your arms and disperse!" he said.

Parker stood rigid, thinking hard. He was not afraid; he would gladly have cried out his defiance. But duty weighed upon him, the duty to his men. It was one thing to sacrifice himself, cry defiance and take the consequences, however dire. But could he sacrifice his men?

Seventy against a thousand! He spared a fleeting glance at the lines, realizing as never before the intimacy of village life, the bonds of kinship. Four of the seventy were Parkers, nine were Harringtons, seven Munroes, three Tidds, three Lockes, three Reeds. Why, they were all woven together into family patterns, like a patchwork quilt, fathers and sons, uncles, nephews and cousins. He realized with a twinge of pain that he loved them—and that at a wrong word from him they might all be slaughtered. Defiance now spelled death.

He turned to face them, and said, "Disperse, men."

They hesitated, fell back a pace, reluctantly, paused—and

heard, somewhere in the British ranks a yell of fury: "Lay down your arms, you damned rebels!"

As if the yell were a signal, the ranks broke, surged and plunged forward, dozens of voices shouting, "Villains, rebels, *scum!* Damn you, lay down your arms!"

The minutemen did not lay down their arms, but their lines wavered.

And in that moment, a shot was fired.

Who had fired it?

John Parker was astounded. Had the explosion come from behind him? No, he thought. The sound had the peculiar whine of a pistol shot. The Lexington company had muskets; the British regulars had rifles. Only the mounted British officers were equipped with pistols.

But the effect of the shot was sudden and disastrous. Like a volcano erupting, the scene dissolved in deafening noise and tumult. Somebody bawled, "Fire, by God, fire! Damn 'em! We'll *have* the traitors now!" A blast from the British guns followed, and was answered by a feeble scattered volley from the militia. As best he could, Parker counted the answering shots; he thought there were seven, or at most eight.

Major Pitcairn jerked his horse about and galloped among his ranks as they swarmed wildly around the green. His horse was nicked in the leg by a flying bullet; it lurched and staggered. The major's sword was pointed downward in the military attitude that commanded the firing to cease.

"Stop!" he shouted frantically. "Stop—"

The command went unheeded. Major Pitcairn's hand was still firm on his horse's bridle, but the rein that controlled his troops had slipped; he could not regain it. At last, at last, the proud redcoats, the elite veterans would even an old score.

And now fear boiled up in John Parker, panic and fear for his men; and he shouted at the top of his lungs: "Fall back! Retreat!" He saw that, beyond the infantry mob, the grenadiers were advancing on the run. Some of the Lexington men were down, dead or wounded. A moment more and escape for the rest would be cut off; they would be killed in their tracks, like cattle.

"*Retreat!*" he begged them. "*Go!*"

They seemed to know their peril, and obeyed him—all except one, Jonas Parker.

Jonas was a cousin of Captain John's. He was fifty-three years old and tough as a thong of deerhide. In his youth, he had been an Indian fighter; yes, and licked the savages, too, in many a scrap! Jonas was fond of his Cousin John. Oh, John was very stanch and reliable. But danged if Jonas would listen to him today!

Retreat? Never!

Jonas put his flint and powder in his hat, and the hat on the ground between his feet, conveniently, so that he wouldn't have to reach for it. He took aim, and a British bullet hit him before he could pull the trigger. He collapsed, but steadied himself on his elbow, grasped his musket tightly, took aim again.

Just as he fired, a British bayonet pierced his heart; he groaned hoarsely and died.

Lieutenant Colonel Smith bustled up from the rear to address Major Pitcairn. He was panting, hot and horrified.

What was happening? Hadn't General Gage specifically said no resort to weapons, no harshness to the countryfolk, no plundering of private property?

Well—look, sir!—your soldiers chasing the Americans from the green, madly pursuing them, shooting at random. And attempting to thrust their way into the church, the houses! Do you see, sir, that fellow yonder in the King's colors, brandishing his rifle at a trembling woman on the threshold of her home?

"Terrible!" fumed Colonel Smith. "Shocking!"

Pitcairn may have wanted to say that the fault was not his alone—"I would have managed the affair more skillfully, Colonel Smith, started from Boston earlier, by a more direct route, wasted no long hours in the swamp at Cambridge, and in needless conferences, arrived here sooner, in time to prevent the alarming of the village, the congregating of the militia"—but a major cannot be as frank as he pleases when talking with a lieutenant colonel. Wisely, Major Pitcairn said nothing.

Colonel Smith collared the straying drummers and told them to drum for all they were worth.

"The rioting must be quelled, the troops recalled to their senses—immediately!"

The drummers made a great din, eventually drowning out the other noises. Gradually, with Colonel Smith's co-operation, Major Pitcairn got the men marshaled into columns. They would, of course, proceed to Concord, announced Colonel Smith; the excursion would be completed according to General Gage's instructions.

So, feeling refreshed and stimulated, the redcoats tramped onward. It was six o'clock, and Concord was five miles away. As they left Lexington, they gave a chorus of loud, lusty cheers, the cheers always given by British regiments after a triumphant engagement.

Once more Captain Parker was counting—casualties now, the damage done to his little band of patriots. Eight killed, ten wounded. The dead were Robert Munroe, Jedediah Munroe, Samuel Hadley, John Brown, Jonas Parker (stubborn old Jonas!), Ashabel Porter, Caleb Harrington—and young Jonathan Harrington who, mortally injured, had crawled and dragged himself across the green, to die on his own doorstep, in the embrace of his weeping wife.

The dead would be buried, and mourned; the wounded tenderly cared for.

Parker saw one dead British soldier, an inert heap of scarlet, lying on the grass near the church: the foreigner also must have a grave, a decent burial. Parker thought that several of the regulars might have been wounded, though he wasn't positive. And Major Pitcairn's horse—he was sure about the horse.

Captain Parker was sad, but not daunted in spirit. His awareness of duty was unshaken, unyielding as iron. This was not an end, it was a beginning. He would reorganize his militia company, enlarge it with new recruits, prepare for the next emergency.

Yes, thought John Parker, something had begun here which must be finished, whatever the cost. England would pay dearly, drop by drop, for the patriot blood spilled on Lexington green. That shot, that first amazing shot splintering the peace of an April morning, would echo east and west, north and south, over a continent, over an ocean, around the world, into the future and down the corridors of time.

2

●●●●●●

The King

It would be weeks before George William Frederick—King George III of England—knew what had occurred at Lexington in the dawn hours of April 19, 1775. A sailing vessel, slowed by adverse winds and waves, would at length bring him letters from General Thomas Gage and other representatives of the Crown in America.

These communications would all stress one significant point. No blame for the "skirmish" could be attributed to any of His Majesty's officers or soldiers. The Lexington militiamen had been the aggressors; brazenly, without provocation, they had opened fire upon a detachment of British troops—who then, of course, had to defend themselves and put the militiamen to flight.

There had also been a little matter at Concord village, of which the full report would be made anon.

At the same time that the pens of the King's correspondents were assiduously scratching, some members of Captain John Parker's company, as well as two or three Lexington civilians, were recollecting and writing down a very different story of the "skirmish." Surely the first shot had not come from a patriot gun! The British had attacked. Yes, one

25

of that howling, murderous mob of redcoats had sparked it all. The British were the aggressors.

Thus was launched a dispute which would continue for decades, a century, and perhaps never be definitely settled.

But to the King, so far away, the fateful day must have seemed quite ordinary. He was a tall, heavily built man of thirty-seven, with powdered hair brushed sleekly down from the top of his head and curled in sausage-like rolls over his ears, a sallow oval countenance, rather protuberant gray eyes and a long straight nose. He wakened to the solid comforts of his London palace; his valet and grooms of the chamber assisted him into his good, somber-colored clothes; he breakfasted with his wife, Queen Charlotte, and his older children.

Now, in 1775, he had three sons and three daughters, and hoped to have more children. A throne must be kept in a family, and this is more easily accomplished in a big family than in a small one. Eventually, George III would be the father of thirteen princes and princesses, all of them plump, round-eyed, in appearance remarkably like himself.

After breakfast, he went as usual about his business, for he had innumerable things to see to: meetings to grace with his royal presence; cabinet officials, envoys and courtiers to interview; tasks that would occupy him until nightfall. A strenuous routine! But he was used to it. He was methodical, industrious, honest and economical. He never indulged in the extravagances that seem to amuse some monarchs. No detail of government was too trifling for his supervision.

He had, in fact, many admirable qualities of character, but in disposition he was vain, obstinate and often sulky. His intellectual interests were limited. He had a degree of curiosity about science, and would have said that he believed in education; he liked music, but cared nothing for art, books or reading—and had been a great hulking boy of eleven before he could read at all.

His physical health was good, but there were times when his memory dimmed, and even failed him. At the age of twenty-seven he had been terribly ill with an obscure sort of mental affliction. Though he had recovered, and his doctors said he would never have a relapse, the thought of that ordeal lingered with him. The remedies applied by the doctors were dreadful—worse, he felt, than the sickness—the canvas jacket into which they strapped him, the solitary confinement in a black-dark room, as if he were a beast they must cage.

Poor man. He had not been permanently cured. He would live to be very old, doomed for the last thirty-two years of life to both insanity and total blindness.

George III had inherited the English throne from his grandfather, George II, who, in turn, had inherited it from his own father, George I. The surname of the Georges was Guelph. They were of German origin, princes of the House of Hanover, a German dynasty.

For almost a century and a half prior to the coming of the Hanoverians, England had been ruled by monarchs of the Stuart family. Queen Anne was the last of the Stuarts. When Anne died in 1714, she was childless: all of her eighteen children had died at birth or in infancy. But in Germany there was George Guelph, the Elector of Hanover, whose grandmother had been a daughter of James I, England's first Stuart king. Since George Guelph had Stuart blood in his veins, he seemed to be Anne's rightful heir—at least no nearer claimant could be found.

So the English throne was offered to the Elector of Hanover. He accepted it with pleasure, and was crowned George I of England.

This George did not speak or understand a word of the English language. He did not like the English people or the climate or the food or the ceremonies of the court. But why bother about these aversions? He was shrewd and scheming. He had been watching England—a small country, but with an expanding foreign trade and colonies in North America.

As king of England, George Guelph could enrich himself and his German properties with English revenue. He selected ministers who would speak the language for him, do his bidding, make the trade more prosperous and give him the lion's share of the profits.

With these objectives, he reigned for thirteen years, spending most of his time and English gold in improving Hanover —and died of a stroke, in his coach, while on a journey there, in 1727.

George II had been born in Germany, and was as German in speech, manners and tastes as his father, but weaker in character. A petty, quarrelsome man, he had been constantly on bad terms with his father, opposing him wherever possible. He quarreled also with his children, and had publicly declared that he hated his oldest son, Frederick, the Prince of Wales. He had no friends, and was sincerely devoted to but one person in the world—his German wife, Queen Caroline—and to but one thing—money.

George II loved money, delighted in fingering it, gloating over the sheen of the metal, the size and weight of the coins. As for the responsibilities of state, somebody else could attend to them! If England was prospering (as seemed, strangely enough, to be the case) it was without help from him. He interfered only when the welfare of Germany and England clashed; then Germany must have his support.

For the thirty-three years that he wore the crown, he was despised by the English people. He outlived the unfortunate

Prince of Wales and knew, as he died in 1760, that his grandson, still another George Guelph, would take his place.

It was in an atmosphere of bitter family feuds that George III grew to manhood. He was English-born; London was his birthplace. He spoke English with some fluency, though with a gruff German accent. He preferred to regard himself as an Englishman, and his concern was more for England than for his lands and titles in Germany.

After the death of his father, George had looked to his mother, Augusta of Saxe-Gotha, Princess of Wales, for guidance. Augusta was a foolish, grasping woman. She had expected that one day she would be the queen of England, and felt that somehow she had been robbed of a splendid career. She was resolved that her son should bask in splendor, and she would enjoy its reflection.

Augusta had noticed that the prestige of the English throne was not what it had been in the Stuart era. George I had been selfish, George II neglectful; the power of the monarch had declined. And as it declined, the power of the ministry and of Parliament strengthened. This might be good for the country, the people, but Augusta saw it as a calamity.

"Be a king, George!" she told the boy—told him frequently, her hand on his shoulder. "God has decreed that you are to rule. From the moment of your crowning, *be a king!*"

Young as he was, he knew just what she meant. He must get back all those rights and prerogatives that the first two Georges had squandered or given away. And having got them back, he must hold on to them.

"Yes, Mother," he said. "I will."

He ascended the throne when he was twenty-two. A king should have a wife, and George was greatly attracted by a beautiful English girl, a lady-in-waiting at his court. Indeed, he was almost in love with the English beauty, imagining her as his queen.

But his mother frowned on the match. "A German princess," Augusta said, "is more suitable."

So the next year he married Princess Charlotte of Mecklenburg.

Though the marriage was to be a happy one for George, and for Charlotte too, his subjects were not well pleased about it. Charlotte was rather dull, dumpy in figure, badly dressed and not pretty at all. George loved her for her meekness and kindness; she was the most amiable of companions. He regretted that she was never a favorite of the English people.

A London cartoonist rashly drew a profile sketch of the royal couple: George in a comical shovel-brimmed hat that shaded his prominent nose; Charlotte, blunt-featured and thick-necked, in a hat resembling a beribboned and veiled pudding bowl. The caption beneath read: *Farmer George and his wife.*

The funny cartoon was not funny to the King; it annoyed him. He didn't enjoy being laughed at (who does?) and he had always been bewildered by the English sense of humor. Why, neither he nor Charlotte looked one bit like the man and woman sketched by the cartoonist!

Yes, he was a farmer—and what of that? He saw to it that his vast fields and vineyards in Hanover were systematically cultivated; he sold his crops, as his ancestors had done, at the best markets, for the highest prices available. He was friendly to the farmers of England, encouraged them in their labors, valued them as a source of the nation's wealth.

He truly wanted the affection of his subjects, needed it and realized that he didn't have it. His marriage had not enhanced his popularity. But he wouldn't quit trying! In his first speech to the Parliament, he told the people how deeply his roots were embedded in the English soil.

"Born and bred in this country, I glory in the name of Briton," he said.

The proud statement was received coolly; the applause was scanty. He felt rebuffed.

Perhaps it was experiences of this sort, little jabs of ridicule such as the cartoon, the impassive faces of his audience in the Parliament, that made him so responsive to his mother's counsel.

The people, he decided, must not be allowed to get above themselves! Oh, he would work for them; they would never have a harder-working or more conscientious king. But they must reward him—if not with affection, then with a proper honoring of his person and his exalted station.

His ministers also must acknowledge him as absolute master. Any cabinet official who did not endorse his policies would be ousted, and a more tractable man substituted. Any old laws that limited his powers would be revoked. Any new laws must have his sanction.

Yes, by the infinite wisdom of God, by divine right, George III was to rule England—and rule he would!

"I will have no innovations in my time!" he said.

With the throne, he had inherited many difficult problems. One that worried him most pertained to his American colonies. He had never visited North America and never intended to; he disliked traveling and in all his life never went farther than a few miles from London. But he had firm ideas as to how his subjects overseas should be managed, for their own good as well as for his.

For the preceding fifty years, even before Queen Anne's reign, England and other European countries had been embroiled in a series of wars with France. The French monarchs Louis XIV, "the Magnificent," and then Louis XV were greedy; they seemed bent upon conquering the universe. Occasionally, there had been short intervals of uncertain peace, but always the conflict was resumed. During the reign of George II, the war spread to America, where it was a struggle between England and France to keep, and if possible to extend, the tremendous stretches of territory which the two nations possessed there.

The French were established in Canada and the upper Mississippi River Valley, and had founded the colony of New Orleans in Louisiana, at the Mississippi's mouth. They planned to link these widely separated holdings with a chain of forts that would reach southward from Lake Erie to the Ohio River, down the Ohio to the Mississippi, and on to the Gulf of Mexico.

England saw the French plan as a menace to her thirteen colonies, and would spare no efforts to thwart it.

When France seized the English trading post at the confluence of the Allegheny and Monongahela, rebuilt it and named it Fort Duquesne, England realized that she must take immediate steps or all her western regions would fall into enemy hands. So, in 1756, the war blazed with renewed fury. This fresh outbreak was known in Europe as the Seven Years' War; in American history, it would be recorded as the French and Indian War, because of the alliance of the northern Indian tribes with France, against the English.

The armies of both countries were valiant, the campaigns long and fiercely contested; but in September, 1759, on the Plains of Abraham, a plateau above the city of Quebec, Canada, the British forces commanded by General James Wolfe decisively defeated the French regiments of the Marquis de Montcalm. With the Battle of Quebec, the conflict in America subsided, though in Europe England and France continued to fight.

It was just a little more than a year after Montcalm's surrender that George II died, bequeathing his crown to his grandson. George III had not been entirely sympathetic with the war; he labeled it as "bloody and expensive"; if he had been on the throne, it might have been avoided! But he rejoiced that the victory was England's and that a treaty signed in Paris in 1763 enormously increased his domain, giving him all of Canada and all other French territory east of the Mississippi, except New Orleans.

Now his colonies were safe from the encroachment of France—and he would save them from the treacherous Indians, too. It seemed that the Indians could not believe that their allies, the French, had been vanquished. The Treaty of Paris? To the Indians, it was nothing more than a scrap of parchment; even as the ink dried on the treaty, they plotted further mischief. Led by the Ottawa chief, Pontiac, they struck at Detroit and recaptured the town and the fort. Throughout the summer of 1763, they burned, destroyed, scalped and murdered, laying waste to the Ohio Valley possessions which the French had forfeited to the English. Pontiac was as clever as he was ruthless. Not until the autumn was his barbaric rebellion put down.

George III felt that his American subjects owed him a great deal for having twice rescued them; he would make sure that they appreciated and paid their debt. All this fighting had drained off huge sums from his treasury; he must be reimbursed for such expenses. He felt also that there must be a resident British army in the colonies, an army large enough to prevent future assaults by the Indians—for who could say that they might not rise again?

Well, more and higher taxes must be levied on the colonists; it was only fair that they should pay for their protection, for feeding and quartering the British soldiers stationed in their towns and villages.

They should be glad to! he thought.

But as time went on, he was disillusioned, and then indignant. The colonists were not glad; they did not appreciate what he had done and was doing for them. On the contrary, they complained about the taxes, the troops—about everything. Why, they were like children—and stupid, ungrateful children at that!

Of course, a family man knows how to handle children. If they're naughty, scold them. If they persist in their naughtiness, punish them severely. It is the only way!

So, on the morning of April 19, 1775, when a sudden shot was fired from a gun (whether English or patriot) at Lexington, Massachusetts, George III was probably thinking of his Americans, for he really never forgot them now. Their naughtiness had become extreme, excruciating; it had taken on the aspect of insurrection. They belonged to him, they were as much his as were the little princes and princesses in the palace nursery. He was a family man, a good father. He had never coddled any of his children, and didn't propose to, either. . . .

"Be a king, George. Be a king!"

3

●●●●●●

The Colonists

In 1763, there were about 1,600,000 people in the thirteen American colonies. If they felt no great indebtedness to their King, it was because they had not sat idly by as witnesses of England's struggle with the French and Indians, but had played a part in it.

Almost since the beginning of their history, the colonies had maintained militia companies, consisting of their able-bodied men, with officers who were commissioned by the royal governors. Every American boy knew that he must serve his stint in the local militia; such service was not begrudged; it was taken for granted as a normal phase of growing to manhood.

The militiamen drilled occasionally, with any weapons they might have at home: muskets, fowling pieces, squirrel guns. Once or twice a year they were paraded for the governor's inspection, while their womenfolk looked on admiringly. In times of danger, the governor could call them out. Often they had repelled Indian forays—a type of warfare in which they acquired the useful knack of sniping and sharpshooting from ambush.

Hundreds of these colonials had been drafted into the

King's army. Marching with the British regulars to Canada or the western forts, they were exposed to the same hardships, battled as bravely, were wounded and in some instances died under the same shell-torn banners.

They might well have said, "We didn't wait to be rescued. We were called—and we answered."

The militia of the northern, or New England, colonies had been especially active in the French and Indian War; but Virginia also had contributed substantial quotas of troops. Virginia was the largest of all the colonies, both in area and population; and it was one of her young officers, George Washington, who earned a degree of fame as an American hero of the war.

George Washington's parents, Augustine and Mary Ball Washington, were Virginians of wealth and social position. Augustine owned and cultivated six plantations. His son George was born in 1732 in the farmhouse of Augustine's Bridges Creek plantation in Westmoreland County.

Most of George's early years were spent at Bridges Creek. He was eleven when his father died, and he came under the guardianship of his half-brother Lawrence. George then went to live at Lawrence's beautiful estate, Mount Vernon, in Fairfax County on the Potomac River.

Lawrence Washington was a gentleman of fashion and education. In his house, George had access to books and obtained some knowledge of Latin and literature. For a while he was a pupil in the neighborhood school, but many things he taught himself.

"I see that you study mathematics," Lawrence said.

"I like it," George answered. "Arithmetic, algebra, geometry. I'm going to be a surveyor."

"A surveyor, eh?" said Lawrence. "Excellent! An excellent profession, Brother."

It was a profession for which George Washington seemed to have much aptitude. At fourteen, he was helping Lawrence to survey and map the Mount Vernon fields. At seventeen, he was made public surveyor of Fairfax County, a job that took him to outlying sections of Virginia and beyond, to the very frontiers of civilization, and gave him resourcefulness, physical endurance and a familiarity with forests and prairies, rivers and lakes and mountains, that would later stand him in good stead.

For three years, he happily pursued his chosen work. Then Lawrence died, leaving a will that named George as his executor, custodian of Mount Vernon and guardian of Mildred Washington, Lawrence's daughter and only child. Mildred was a delicate girl, she did not long survive her father. At her death, the property that had come to her from Lawrence—the fertile acres of Mount Vernon, the slaves and the big house—passed to George's ownership.

He was a young man of twenty and rather bewildered at facing a life that had so swiftly changed its pattern.

And more changes were in store for him. Scarcely had he got his household and the plantation smoothly running, and been elected to the vestry of the Episcopal Church in which his family had always worshiped, and taken on other obligations of a good citizen in Fairfax County, than the French war loomed.

In 1755, Governor Dinwiddie of Virginia called out the colony's militia, appointed George Washington as a major and sent him to warn the French that they must stop their invasion of the Ohio Valley. In 1755, Washington was promoted to the rank of lieutenant colonel, commander of all the Virginia forces and aide to the British general, Edward Braddock, who was directing the western campaigns.

Colonel Washington was not yet twenty-four years old— but a fine figure of a man in his blue-and-buff continental uniform. He was tall, strong, vigorous, rather shy, never very talkative, but as courteous to his subordinates as to his superiors. It would be said of him that he didn't win every battle in which he engaged; sometimes the odds were overwhelmingly against him and he was defeated. But invariably, in defeat or in triumph, he showed an unflinching gallantry that inspired his men to follow him.

And he didn't mind soldiering. It wasn't a bad existence. In a letter to a relative, he wrote: "I have heard the bullets whistle; and, believe me, there is something charming in the sound."

The blithe comment reached the ears of his British comrades-in-arms, and at length was repeated to the King and the cabinet ministers in London. The ministers smiled; the King was sarcastic.

"Charming?" said the King. "This youth is a braggart."

Colonel Washington had been charmed by a lady, too. With the close of the war in 1759, he resigned his commission, went back to Virginia and married Martha Dandridge Custis, a rich young widow whom he had met a year previously. Martha was just his age; she was sweet, cheerful, pretty; he knew she would be the perfect wife for him.

Martha brought him a fortune in land and slaves—and a little son and daughter, the children of her first marriage. He combined Martha's land with his and developed it all with strict economy. The Custis children he welcomed and loved; indeed, he loved all children, and had an almost magical way of gaining their confidence and affection.

Now the future seemed to stretch pleasantly and serenely before him. He had no soaring ambitions. He was content to be a farmer, superintending the slaves as they sowed and harvested his crops of tobacco and grain, or pruned his luxurious fruit orchards.

He disapproved of slavery, not so much on moral grounds,

but as an impractical system; he thought it finally would have to be discarded. Free labor was infinitely better. But slavery was the system of the southern American colonies, so old and entrenched that he knew of nothing to be done about it, except to see that the Washington Negroes were well cared for.

He enjoyed recreation and entertainment, and had the leisure for them. Riding, fox hunting, picnics, clambakes and barbecues, amateur theatricals—he liked them all. And dancing? Why, there wasn't a more agile or untiring dancer in the county! He could dance the night away, until the fiddlers yawned and the candles winked out in their drippings. He was a generous host and Martha a cordial hostess. The latchstring at Mount Vernon was always out, the doors open to parties of guests who might stay a week, a month or a season.

He seemed to have found the path from which he was never to deviate, and it was not surveying, not soldiering, but farming. An American "Farmer George and his wife." No more changes!

And yet in his heart he was doubtful.

What of other people? This contentment he felt—wasn't it a personal satisfaction? Not everyone, perhaps only a lucky few, were so blessed.

He was a member of the House of Burgesses, the legislative body of Virginia. As a representative of Fairfax County, he went to the sessions in Williamsburg, the Virginia capital. He listened to the debates. It was all too apparent that unrest was in the wind, a lurking distrust of the King and Parliament. He listened to the speeches of Patrick Henry, the member from Hanover County.

Patrick Henry was a lawyer, a radical in politics, an orator so eloquent that he could sway a crowd to fervent applause. He was impulsive, rash; sometimes his statements were grossly exaggerated. But when he spoke his audiences were breathless, leaning forward, anxious not to miss a word.

Patrick Henry said that the King of England had become a tyrant. Since George III had mounted the throne, the colonists had been in sorry plight. He listed their grievances, the new taxes, the harsher trade regulations. Each of the colonies had its legislature—but of what good were laws made by these legislatures if they could be annulled, arrogantly set aside by the King and Parliament?

The sad truth was, said Patrick Henry, that the King scorned the American colonies; they were to him merely a source of revenue. The logical conclusion was that he no longer deserved their homage. Would Virginians submit to being exploited and abused? Or would they decide to legislate for themselves, independently of England?

In this period, shortly after the French and Indian War and the Treaty of Paris, George Washington was slowly sorting out his political beliefs. He was not impulsive, and he never exaggerated; he was thoughtful. Probably his opinions were more in accord with those expressed by another colonial lawyer, James Otis of Boston.

James Otis had published pamphlets and essays which many thoughtful Americans were reading and pondering. God had made all men naturally equal, wrote Otis. Government was instituted for the benefit of the governed. A government that was harmful to the people should be opposed. The American colonists were British subjects, as much so as the inhabitants of the British Isles, as much so as if they lived in the shadow of Westminster Palace. Therefore they were entitled to all the rights allowed to British subjects nearer home, rights which now were shrinking, vanishing. They were entitled to representation in the Parliament; if that concession was made to them, all would be well.

But it must be remembered, Otis cautiously concluded,

that the King was still the monarch; Parliament the supreme power. Relief for the American colonists' condition must come through the workings of Parliament and those cabinet ministers who were friendly to the colonists' cause.

George Washington would examine the rapidly widening breach between England and her colonies from every angle, and arrive—slowly—at his own conclusions. He was not in theory opposed to monarchy as a form of government; he could not quite visualize a different form.

Patrick Henry's "independence"—what was it? What did it mean? Were the colonies to break all ties with the Crown? What would become of them then? They must have something to grapple them together. What would that something be?

To have a king meant to have order—and was not order the prime requisite of life?

But Washington hated injustice of any kind; it was abhorrent to him. And he was unselfish. Oh, yes, he was of course a British subject; but America was his country. He must always respond to any rightful demand made upon him by his fellow Americans.

So his thoughts moved slowly, gravely, toward a decision.

4

●●●●●●

A Remarkable Man

However King George might judge the American colonists, they knew that they were not stupid, ungrateful children—or children at all. And did he think that they didn't appreciate him? Perhaps the shoe was on the other foot and it was the King who lacked a proper appreciation of *them*—their strength, their value to his realm.

The colonists realized, if the King did not, that the French and Indian War had affected them financially. Though they had made sacrifices for it, they had profited by it, too.

All wars are costly to the nations that wage them. To carry on any war, a great deal of money must be spent to supply the armies, and the civilians who manufacture or sell such supplies are certain to become prosperous.

So it had been with England and the colonies. For her long conflict with the French, and then with Pontiac, England had transported thousands of soldiers, tons of ammunition and cannon, but she could not send everything needed for the soldiers' day-to-day subsistence. Immense quantities of provisions of many kinds had to be bought nearer the scene of the fighting—bought from American farmers, traders and artisans.

As a result, business in the colonies had boomed, old industries expanded, new manufacturing started. A majority of the people were better-off financially than ever they were before. This prosperity altered their outlook on the world and gave them a nice feeling of importance.

Also the war had taught them the lesson of co-operation. Their small, separate companies of troops had been forged into a sizable army that was of great help in the conquering of England's foes. Some bold Americans dared to ask themselves whether this didn't indicate that they could, if they should have to, muster such an army to conquer foes of their own.

"The war," they said, "has shown us our kinship. Aren't we all the descendants of pioneers who carved out a new civilization from the primitive wilderness? Can the British subject in England really understand the life we lead here, the country we're building, and hope to build?"

Somehow a man in Virginia or the Carolinas felt closer now to the Rhode Islander, the New Yorker, the man in Delaware or New Hampshire, than to his cousins across the Atlantic.

Benjamin Franklin of Philadelphia was one of the first among them to perceive and to suggest the worth of united effort.

In the spring of 1754, Franklin printed in his newspaper, the *Pennsylvania Gazette,* a woodcut picture of a snake divided from head to tail into eight pieces. Each piece had on it the initials of a colony or group of colonies: New England, New York, New Jersey, Pennsylvania, Maryland, Virginia, North Carolina, South Carolina. Beneath the severed snake was the admonition: *Join, or Die.*

The picture was copied in colonial papers everywhere. The phrase was one to catch the eye and stick in the memory.

In June of that year, when the French were stirring up the Indians, Franklin went as a delegate from Pennsylvania to a meeting at Albany, New York, called for the purpose of making a peace treaty with the six tribes of the Iroquois League. Unlike many Indians, the Iroquois had always been friendly to the English settlers, and meeting now with these emissaries from the eastern colonies, they agreed to keep the peace.

But Franklin had something else, and more, for the delegates to consider: a plan of union, afterward known as the Albany Plan.

"I propose," Franklin said, "a confederation, with a president appointed by the Crown and a grand council to which the legislatures or assemblies of all our colonies will elect representatives. The president's salary will be paid by the Crown. The grand council will be a central governing body —but making only such laws as are approved by the president and the King."

The delegates discussed Franklin's plan and voted to adopt it; but when they took it back to their legislatures, it was rejected.

A central government? The idea was too novel, too different, a little frightening. The legislatures, one and all, voted against it. And the King, when informed of the Albany Plan, said it was utter foolishness and never, *never*, would have the consent of the Crown.

As for Franklin's reaction to this rebuff, he said he had rather expected it. "We don't know each other yet," he said. "We must get better acquainted."

Benjamin Franklin was then forty-eight years old, postmaster general for the English colonies, the most famous man in America, one of the most remarkable men his country would ever produce.

He had been born in Boston where his father, Josiah, was a soap-boiler and candle-maker. Benjamin was the youngest boy in a big family. The Franklins were plain people, in modest circumstances, but intelligent and with some education.

At the age of ten, Benjamin was apprenticed to his father, but he didn't like soap-boiling and wrinkled his nose in disgust at the stuffy atmosphere of the tallow shed. He was fascinated by the sea; he dreamed of being a sailor. His father, fearful that he might run away, apprenticed him to an older brother, James, who was a printer.

Benjamin quickly learned the printer's trade; it was easy for him. James published a newspaper, the *New England Courant*, in his shop, and now Benjamin dreamed of writing for the paper.

"Writing what?" said James, when the notion was broached to him. "Your chores, my lad, are sweeping the floor, cleaning type and distributing the *Courant* to subscribers."

Benjamin worked briskly in the shop, but he had interests, dozens of them, outside it. What a place the world was, teeming with exciting things to do and learn! Maybe he couldn't do and learn them all, but it would not be for want of trying.

He loved to read; his every spare penny went to buy books, which he read over and over again. He was athletic, proficient at games, and such a fine swimmer that he once thought of advertising as a swimming instructor. And he did want to write! Often, secretly and just for fun, he dashed off little verses or attempted squibs and articles in the style of the English essayists Addison and Steele.

He worked for James until he was seventeen. James was a surly, brutish fellow. Frequently the brothers quarreled—at last seriously. It was a prank of Benjamin's that brought about the climax.

For several weeks he had been writing letters to the *Courant,* signing them with the fictitious name of "Silence Dogood," and slipping them under the shop door, for James to find.

Silence Dogood described herself as the respectable widow of a country parson, the mother of three children, a lady who "had the instinct to observe and reprove the faults of others." Her letters were concerned with the faults of the Bostonians she was now observing: the bad manners of the students at Harvard College, the tendency of Boston gentlemen to drink too much, the flirtatious ways of young women promenading on Boston Common in the evenings, the hypocritical preachers and churchgoers who weren't half so religious as they claimed to be!

James Franklin was amused by Silence Dogood. He was satirical by nature; he detested reformers of the "respectable widow's" sort. He suspected that the letters were not genuine, that Silence was an impostor making sport of all "dogooders"; but she was saying many things that James would have liked to say himself. He printed fourteen of her letters and knew that people read them eagerly—indeed, they were the talk of the town.

Benjamin was amused also, and delighted. Each letter was wittier that the one preceding, as Benjamin sharpened his pen and his prose style. Sometimes he could hardly write for laughing at his own cleverness. Silence Dogood was so real to him that he almost believed she truly existed.

But inevitably the day came when Mrs. Dogood—and Benjamin—were unmasked, their identities revealed. Then James was irate. He had thought that his mysterious correspondent must be a man: no woman in Boston could write so well, so ironically; but he had never guessed his brother—his lowly, grubby apprentice—had such ability.

James grabbed Benjamin by the collar, shook him till his

teeth rattled, boxed his ears. "Scoundrel, deceiver, you tricked me!" he roared.

Benjamin was dismayed. James had cuffed him about before, but never so viciously. "You liked the letters, James—"

"You liar!" James shook him again. "You little worm!"

Benjamin snatched off his leather apron. "I'm through," he said. "I'm leaving."

James sneered. "You can't leave. You're my apprentice, under contract to me. Leave? If you did, not another printer in Boston would ever hire you."

"Boston is not the only city in America," Benjamin said. "I'm going."

He did not leave immediately. His father intervened, begged him to wait, to make it up with James. But the brothers could not work together now; Benjamin was resentful, James scowling, waspish and perhaps a little jealous.

On September 30, 1723, this item appeared in the *Courant:* "James Franklin, Printer in Queen Street, wants a likely lad for an apprentice."

Benjamin went to Philadelphia and got work in a print-shop there. He was a shabby young stranger in a strange town; but his sunny disposition, his good sense and talents soon drew friends to him. His success in the next few years, and afterward, was phenomenal.

At twenty-three, he was owner and editor of the *Pennsylvania Gazette* and, as a side line, was annually publishing his *Poor Richard's Almanack.* American housewives had always bought almanacs—such handy things to have hanging in the kitchen—but Franklin's far outsold others printed in the colonies. His paperbound booklet contained not only the usual information on changes in the moon and the tides, and weather predictions, but recipes, jokes, jingling rhymes and salty proverbs.

"Poor Richard" was a philosopher. His original sayings were read, smiled at, quoted. Many would be preserved in a nation's folklore:

God helps them that help themselves.
Little strokes fell great oaks.
A cat with gloves catches no mice.
Plough deep while sluggards sleep.
Early to bed and early to rise makes a man healthy, wealthy and wise.

Benjamin Franklin went early to bed; he was an early riser and ploughed deep while sluggards slept; he was healthy and quite wise, but it was the *Almanack* that made him wealthy. With the earnings from it, he extended his publishing business, establishing branches in New York and Charleston, South Carolina, even in such remote spots as the British West Indies. He was an organizer, an inventor, a discoverer; and by the time he reached the age of forty, the people of Philadelphia hailed him as their foremost citizen, their beloved "Mr. Ben."

He organized social and scholarly clubs, the University of Pennsylvania, the first circulating library in America, the first fire company, the first public mail service. He invented a marvelous new stove for heating houses, a new kind of draft for fireplaces, a device to cure chimneys of smoking, bifocal lenses for spectacles, a musical instrument that he called the "armonica." He made the amazing discovery that lightning and electricity are the same thing! Then he invented the lightning rod to avert lightning's destruction.

His experiments with electricity were reported in American scientific journals, translated into foreign languages and published throughout Europe.

"How convenient," he said, "if I could read and speak some of these languages! I must learn them."

So he got Latin, French, Italian and Spanish grammars, studied them and became a sprightly linguist.

As one of Philadelphia's city councilmen, and as clerk and then a member of the Pennsylvania Assembly, he was interested in politics. In 1753, he took office as colonial postmaster general.

The French and Indian War was just beginning. Franklin knew that Pennsylvania would be embroiled in it, and he formulated his plan of union by which all the colonies might have been safeguarded. When nothing came of the plan, he looked about for some other means of assisting the war effort.

The colony of Pennsylvania was founded by the Quaker philanthropist William Penn as a refuge for people who suffered religious persecution in Europe. William Penn was an immensely rich Englishman; his motives were pure and sincere. The English Quakers and the Protestants of Germany flocked to him in large numbers. He promised them freedom of worship in America, almost complete self-government and peaceful relations with the Indians, whom he had placated with gifts and kindness.

While William Penn lived, these pleasant conditions prevailed in his colony; but his sons and heirs, Thomas and Richard, were devoid of their saintly parent's idealism. The younger Penns sent despotic royal governors to Pennsylvania and refused to pay the taxes lawfully assessed by the assembly on their vast holdings there. In 1755, they would not lift a finger or give a farthing toward the defense of Pennsylvania against the French and Indian onslaughts.

Benjamin Franklin, believing as he did in co-operation, was troubled by the colony's predicament. Braddock, the British general, had arrived in America and was encamped at Frederick, Maryland, preparing to campaign in the Ohio Valley. Other colonies were providing Braddock with militia troops or with money for his army. Pennsylvania offered him neither.

"And why is Pennsylvania so remiss?" Braddock inquired.

He was told that most Pennsylvanians were Quakers, whose religious principles forbade their being soldiers; gradually the colony's militia had dwindled into oblivion. As for money, the public treasury had no funds, Thomas and Richard Penn would contribute none, and the well-to-do bankers and merchants of Pennsylvania would not donate, for fear of offending their Quakers customers.

"Absurd!" said Braddock. "Disgraceful!"

When Franklin heard about Braddock's comment, he thought of Poor Richard's adage in the *Almanack: God helps them that helps themselves.* Franklin knew the Pennsylvania bankers and merchants, as he knew everyone. He went to them and arranged for them to lend the assembly a sum of money, to be sent to Braddock. Then he went to Frederick, to see that the money had been received.

General Braddock greeted Postmaster General Franklin politely. "I must thank you, sir," he said. "But Pennsylvania should thank you even more."

Franklin smiled. "My visit is not official. I'm here as a private citizen."

"Well, you must dine with me," said Braddock, "and be introduced to my staff."

At the general's table that night, Franklin met Colonel George Washington, Braddock's aide. He shook hands with the tall young Virginian.

"Colonel Washington, you have been mentioned and praised for your courage in the columns of my paper, the *Gazette,*" he said. As Colonel Washington bowed and blushed, Franklin turned to Braddock and said in an undertone, "I have a quick eye to recognize merit when I see it. This is an exceptional young man."

"Very," said Braddock. "He will go far."

During the meal, Braddock said rather fretfully that he was stranded in Frederick. He needed wagons—how else was he to move his gear? Must his soldiers lug the cannon on their backs?

"And your American roads, Mr. Franklin! They are a scandal, not roads at all."

Franklin nodded. "Yes, yes, our roads are bad and the terrain rugged. You say you need wagons?"

"And horses. Or mules, oxen, elephants, any large animal on four legs. And drivers for them. But they're not to be had."

"I can get them for you," Franklin said.

"What!"

"I shall have them for you in a fortnight, sir."

Hurrying from the camp, Franklin scoured Pennsylvania, bargained with the German farmers for wagons and horses. If the farmers would not sell on credit, Franklin delved into his pocket for cash. In exactly two weeks, he was again in Frederick with one hundred and fifty wagons, a team and driver for each of them.

Braddock set out at once for Ohio. Franklin, in Philadelphia, waited for news of his triumphs. But the bulletin brought to him by messenger in July was woeful. At Fort Duquesne, the British had been surprised, crushed, routed, and General Braddock mortally wounded.

"Colonel Washington was with him when he died," the messenger said. "Washington was not hurt. It was only by his skill in directing the retreat that the army was not demolished."

Braddock's disaster terrified Pennsylvania. The assembly convened and voted to create a militia. Benjamin Franklin was commissioned as a colonel and charged with fortifying the colony's western border. The task was dangerous, grueling; for months Franklin and his green militiamen toiled at it, building forts in the border towns.

Then the assembly decided that Richard and Thomas Penn must somehow be persuaded of their obligation to stand by and support the colony before the allied French and Indians overran and ravaged it. An envoy must be sent to interview them in London.

Of course, Benjamin Franklin was the person to send.

He went to London in the spring of 1757. He saw the Penns, and after several interviews and months of patient argument, he wrung from them a pledge to pay at least a fraction of the sum they owed the Pennsylvania treasury. And having done so, he stayed on in England for more than four years.

The British people knew few Americans, but this one they knew by reputation and by his writings, and they warmly welcomed him. Scientists and scholars sought him out to ask him about his electrical investigations and inventions. He chatted with statesmen, with cabinet ministers. He traveled to Scotland, and there the University of St. Andrews bestowed upon him the honorary degree of doctor of laws.

Dr. Franklin? He liked the title and would use it.

In 1761 he made a tour of Holland, talked with Dutch scientists, lectured to Dutch students. Then, in the autumn, he went back home to Philadelphia.

He had seen George III crowned King of England. He believed in and revered the monarchy. His ancestors all had been English; he thought of himself as a British subject—a British subject who lived in and loved America. He hoped, and optimistically believed, that this young George III would be a better king than old George II, his grandfather, had been; that he would be a good friend to the colonists, giving them more voice in government, better royal governors, representation in the Parliament.

Franklin had been a long time absent from his native land, out of touch with his own people. He did not know that now some Americans were thinking of a possible future in which their country might be self-sustaining, quite apart from any king or Parliament.

5

●●●●●●

The Stamp Act

George III donned his crown, not as the benevolent king Dr. Benjamin Franklin had hoped for, but as one bent on ruling with an iron hand—and never mind the velvet glove! His dominion would be absolute; his subjects and cabinet alike must realize the fact.

The war with France, which he had thought of as an extravagance, was now ended in America, but conditions there were not what they should be. The colonists were exhibiting a certain pride and impertinence. To keep them submissive, they must be kept poor.

In the last years of George II's reign, Sir William Pitt had been England's minister of foreign affairs. Pitt was a most capable statesman, but inclined to be sympathetic toward Americans; for this sentiment, he lost his place in George III's cabinet. An added fault of Sir William Pitt's was his great popularity with the people. If Englishmen, whether at home or abroad, were looking for someone to laud and idolize, let them look to the throne!

The new minister of foreign affairs was Sir George Grenville, who saw eye-to-eye with the King on all matters.

For a long time, England had restricted the commerce of

the colonies by laying heavy duties on goods shipped to American markets; and for almost as long, many American importers had evaded the duties by smuggling. The Crown's customs officials had been repeatedly told to stop this violation of the law, but they had not succeeded in doing so. Smugglers were often arrested, but when tried in colonial courts were usually acquitted. As a consequence, the smugglers had persisted, and the frustrated customs men were prone to ignore them.

Now Lord Grenville said that all such offenders would be caught, convicted and fined or imprisoned, probably both.

"The law is the law," said Grenville pompously, "and I will prove that it can be enforced."

In 1761, search warrants of a special sort were issued to the customs officials. The warrants were known as "writs of assistance." Armed with one of them, the officials could seize and confiscate any shipment of wares unloaded at a colonial dock. The contents of the bales, boxes and barrels might be contraband, or might not; it was enough if the official said they were.

American merchants protested immediately that the writs were unfair, giving the customs men arbitrary power. "Suppose the official is unscrupulous?" they asked angrily. "What's to prevent his abusing this power?"

To Patrick Henry of Virginia the writs were an opportunity for setting forth his political views, material for his eloquence and love of liberty. All was grist that came to Patrick Henry's mill! Tall, thin, a bit stooped, with an angular face and the piercing glance of an eagle, he was attaining prominence as a lawyer. Many clients brought cases to him, and he tried the cases competently; but always during the court proceedings he got around to pleading another cause, the one nearest his heart—the rights of the colonists to justice at the King's hands.

And while Patrick Henry was still denouncing the writs of assistance, Lord Grenville obtained Parliament's passage of the Stamp Act. This act, which would become effective in November, 1765, levied a tax on legal documents in the colonies, on printed books, newspapers, playing cards and similar articles.

"A mild act, a slight tax," said Lord Grenville, and he assured the King that the Americans were unlikely to object to it—or to notice one feature of it, that persons accused of disobedience might not have the benefit of trial by jury.

The colonists who were angry before were now furious. They hated the Stamp Act; nothing had ever so incensed them. A slight tax? Yes, but what about the penalty for not paying it? Trial by jury was a basic privilege, guaranteed to British subjects for centuries. The Stamp Act must be repealed!

In May, when the Virginia House of Burgesses was in session at Williamsburg, Patrick Henry assailed the Stamp Act in his inimitable way. His speech was fiery, tempestuous; he gestured dramatically, his deep voice reverberated: *"Caesar had his Brutus, Charles the First his Cromwell, and George the Third—"*

Some of the more cautious burgesses blinked, shifted in their chairs, interrupted. "Treason," they muttered. "Treason."

Patrick Henry paused—only for a moment. Then, unabashed, he cried: *"And George the Third may profit by their example. If this be treason, make the most of it!"*

The cautious burgesses frowned. What, really, was Henry suggesting? Rebellion? They meditated. There were in Virginia, as in all the colonies, many people whose belief in the monarchy was so ingrained that they would never openly oppose it, no matter how arrantly it treated them. Was Patrick Henry saying too much, going too far?

But later in the session, a majority of the burgesses voted not to comply with the Stamp Act, and to adopt the "Virginia Resolves," framed by Henry, which asserted the right of the colonies to independent government.

Condemnation of the Stamp Act was widespread, but noisier, more vehement in Boston than anywhere else. Boston was an old town, with old-fashioned traditions. Most of its twenty thousand inhabitants were staid and sober folk, but there was a rougher element of day-laborers, journeymen, sailors, rope-makers, fishermen and porters who seemed to thrive on turmoil.

These boisterous Bostonians had often rioted. Now, led by a bullying cobbler named Mackintosh, they paraded almost nightly, demanding repeal of the Stamp Act, yelling and hooting, throwing stones, breaking windows. Sir Francis Bernard, the royal governor of Massachusetts was dismayed by their demonstrations—and then so frightened that he ran for his life.

"Well," said Mackintosh to his followers, "if we can't get the governor, we'll take next best, the lieutenant-governor, Tom Hutchinson!"

Thomas Hutchinson was himself a Bostonian, born and bred, and a member of the Massachusetts legislature. He was rich; his fine house was surrounded by fences and gardens. His wife had died and he had not remarried; he had five children to whom he was the fondest of fathers. He was a historian and for several years had been writing the history of Massachusetts colony, a work of absorbing interest to him.

In the past, the town had held Thomas Hutchinson somewhat in awe as a distinguished citizen, an aristocrat, an honorable man, though rather haughty and aloof. But as lieutenant-governor, he was an agent of the King's.

"Therefore," said the cobbler Mackintosh, "he must be *got!*"

On the night of August 26, 1765, a hot summer night, Hutchinson, his children and five servants were in his house when his sister, Mrs. Mather, rushed in upon them.

"Oh, Thomas!" Mrs. Mather exclaimed. "Mackintosh is coming here! Mackintosh and his mob, as wild and drunk as they can be! You must leave at once, come home with me!"

Hutchinson was perturbed and yet self-possessed. "I'll not be turned out of my house by Mackintosh, Sister," he said. "But if you will look after the children—"

"Yes, yes!" said Mrs. Mather. "Come, children."

Hutchinson's three sons, half-grown boys, said they would not leave. "We'll stay with Father," they said. "We'll barricade the doors!"

"And I'll stay!" said Sallie, the older of the two girls.

"Sallie," Hutchinson said, "go with your aunt—"

"I won't!" Sallie cried. "If you die in this room, I'll die with you!"

The windows were open; Hutchinson could hear the mob approaching, the clump of boots, ribald shouts and singing. Sallie was sobbing hysterically; Mrs. Mather wept and sobbed. A trembling servant entered the room to say that men were in the garden, pulling down the trellises and arbors. They were at the back door and at the front, with axes.

Sallie screamed.

"Hush," Hutchinson said. "We'll all leave, Sallie. We'll get a carriage and go out to the farm."

The doors fell to the axes. The mob wrecked the house and everything in it: furniture, rugs, draperies, family portraits; china and glass were smashed; money, jewelry and silverplate stolen; the cupboards emptied of food, the cellars of wine. Hutchinson's library was rifled, his books burned, the manuscript of his history torn to shreds, and the shreds flung into the street.

By morning, the house was only a skeleton of floors and bare walls, the slate roof pried off, the ornamental cupola toppled into the shrubbery.

The Boston rioters had one leader who never paraded, yelled or ruined property, but remained well in the background. His name was Samuel Adams. A graduate of Harvard College, he had studied law, but never practiced it. He had failed in several business ventures, and in 1765 had no steady employment.

Samuel Adams was middle-aged, gray-haired, of medium height. He had a palsy that made his head and hands quiver; his clothes were cheap and untidy. He looked, and was, hard-up, down-at-heel, out-at-elbow, and little did he care! His mind was keen and quick, and he knew it. He was passionately hostile to England, George III, all kings, all royal authority and dedicated to the theory that the American colonies must have complete freedom.

This was his goal, his obsession, his life. He desired and thought of nothing beyond it.

At one time he had been Boston's tax collector, a job to which he could not have been less suited. When poverty-stricken people told him they couldn't pay their taxes, he said: "Just forget about them." This generosity had made it possible for him to build and to control, though very quietly, a strong political machine, which controlled elections in Boston. But he never sought political plums for himself. He preferred to keep behind the scenes, manipulating the strings, while others strutted in the limelight. He was utterly devoid of personal greed.

Samuel Adams watched the young men who were coming to the fore in the community, made friends among them and chose the brightest and best as his boon companions. He was like a spider snaring flies. Into his web, his circle of intimates, he drew his second cousin, John Adams, and John Hancock, both of whom were Harvard graduates: John Adams a lawyer from the nearby village of Braintree, blunt in manner, fearless, honest to the very bones; John Hancock a merchant and importer, the richest man in Massachusetts. Also in Samuel Adams's circle was the handsome, idealistic young physician Dr. Joseph Warren, the Boston silversmith Paul Revere, and perhaps a dozen more earnest and energetic patriots.

These close associates were seldom in the ranks of the mob. They were off-stage, in the wings with Adams, sharing his ardor, relying on his guidance. He had faith in them and in himself, never doubting his fitness as a guide.

As much as any man in America, Samuel Adams would influence the destiny of the colonies in the next few years.

In 1765, Benjamin Franklin was again in London. Thomas and Richard Penn had not fulfilled their pledge, and Pennsylvania floundered in a sea of financial problems. The assembly had sent Dr. Franklin back for more persuading.

Franklin had not complained about the Stamp Act; indeed, he had thought rather well of it. If the colonies must be further taxed, this seemed to him a moderate method. The stamps really weren't expensive, and since they were something everybody would have to buy at one time or another (but the wealthy, who could afford them, more often than the poor) the tax didn't discriminate against either class; nobody's purse would be seriously dented.

So Franklin had thought. But now he wondered. Letters came to him from home, hundreds of letters. Astonishing letters! Why, the colonists were in a perfect uproar over the Stamp Act!

He read about Patrick Henry's speech to the burgesses at Williamsburg, the Virginia Resolves, the Boston riots, the sacking of Thomas Hutchinson's mansion. The letters said that Samuel Adams and his cronies had organized a secret society, the Sons of Liberty, to oppose all tyrannical measures. Now New York and New Jersey had Sons of Liberty societies; the groups sprang up almost overnight, like toadstools!

Liberty? The word seemed to be on the lips and rippling from the pens of all Americans. In Boston there was a towering elm tree called the Liberty Tree; the space beneath its branches was Liberty Hall, a rendezvous for the Boston rabble. Other colonial towns were christening their "liberty trees." On village greens "liberty poles" were being set up as rallying centers. Peaked caps known as "liberty caps" were the newest mode in headgear.

Liberty? A beautiful word—and apparently as contagious as a fever.

In October, a Stamp Act Congress was held in New York City. Delegates from nine colonies signed resolutions that declared, as Virginians already had done, that the colonists could not be taxed except by their own legislatures, where alone they were represented.

In November, the Stamp Act went into effect—but such small effect! New Yorkers flatly said they wouldn't buy the odious stamps, or import any English commodities until the act was repealed. In Connecticut and New Jersey, the stamp distributors appointed by Parliament were threatened with damage to themselves and their shops. Bostonians, afraid of the mobs, were afraid of the stamps too.

Benjamin Franklin brooded. Yes, the Stamp Act was a mistake; it endangered peace and must be repealed. He would work for its repeal. He was not in his usual high feather—

he had the gout. His feet ached when he walked. But gout would not deter him.

He looked up all his old friends in London, enlisted their help. He cultivated acquaintance with cabinet ministers, visited and besieged them with reasons for erasing the obnoxious act from the statutes.

"Repeal?" said the statesmen. "It would be an intricate process, Dr. Franklin."

"But can it be accomplished?" he asked.

"There is a chance," the statesmen replied. "A meager chance."

He called on British manufacturers and shippers, reminding them that by the loss of sales in America their profits would be diminished. He wrote articles and got them printed in English newspapers and periodicals.

But something more was required, he thought. A cartoon, a picture; any situation can be better understood if it's seen as a picture.

Accordingly, he had a cartoon made and engraved on little cards. He distributed the cards as handbills, enclosed them with the writings he sent to publishers.

The cartoon was hideous. It portrayed a woman whose arms and legs had been slashed from her body. The woman was England; the severed arms and legs at which she gazed with anguished eyes were the colonies, Virginia and Pennsylvania, New York and New England.

Poor woman! How could she survive such dreadful mutilation?

At the Albany convention, so long ago, Franklin's cartoon of the snake had warned the colonies to *Join, or Die*. Now he was saying, in substance, that neither England nor the colonies could live without the other, but for the sake of both must unite as a healthy, harmonious whole.

The English people knew Dr. Benjamin Franklin; they

understood his cartoon. This big stout American with the benign countenance and genial smile had become a familiar figure in London. He was no radical, he was loyal to the King—what Dr. Franklin said should be heeded!

So the people were for him; and as the weeks went by, his crusade gained support, of an odd kind, in another quarter.

Lord Grenville had vexed the King. Yes, George III was in a temper. Hadn't Grenville said the colonists would accept the Stamp Act without whimpering? And what had happened? A tempest in America, a tornado, and the stamps unsold, a drug on the market!

Lord Grenville had blundered, and the King was not fond of blunderers, did not easily forgive them. Besides, Grenville was a prodigious bore, always reciting anecdotes that he seemed to think were comical, but to the King were dry as dust. The King had no stomach for British comedy; he was tired of Lord Grenville. Away with the dull, deceitful fellow! Get rid of him!

In January, 1766, Franklin was summoned to Parliament to answer questions of members of the House of Commons about the Stamp Act agitation in America. He dressed carefully for the occasion: a skirted, plum-colored coat, knee breeches, a ruffled shirt and flowered silk waistcoat, white stockings and buckled shoes; his wig was powdered white as snow. With his spectacles a little askew on his nose, but with dignity and poise, he walked into the House of Commons and took his seat.

"What is your name and abode, sir?"

"Franklin, of Philadelphia," he said.

"You know that the colonists have not consented to the Stamp Act?"

"Yes. I know they will never consent to this tax or any tax until they are represented in Parliament."

"But if we lay a tax on the very necessities of life, Dr. Franklin, what then?"

"I do not know of a single thing the colonies need that they cannot produce in America," he replied.

"They buy great quantities of cloth from England. Would it not be some time before they could manufacture cloth?"

"Yes, but it can be done. Before the colonists have worn out their clothes, they will have new ones—of American wool. Our people have said they will eat no lamb, so that the supply of wool may be increased. In three years, we will have an abundance of wool."

"Dr. Franklin, how can the colonies be compelled to pay this stamp tax? Must an army be sent over to enforce it?"

He paused. "British soldiers are already in America," he said. "Suppose more are sent, an army? They will not find an army in the colonies. Nor can they compel a man to buy or use the stamps if he wishes not to. British troops will not find a rebellion in America—but they may make one."

For three hours, he answered the questions clearly, concisely. He had prepared himself well. His inquisitors were members of Parliament friendly to him—indeed, they had told him what he probably would be asked. Then the meeting was adjourned, and he went back to his hotel.

In the taproom, drinking a tankard of ale, he was suddenly conscious of his gout. His miserable feet, how they ached! And all day he had quite forgotten about them!

On February 22, Parliament repealed the Stamp Act. London crowds cheered the announcement. When the news reached America, the colonists celebrated exuberantly, ringing church bells, lighting bonfires. Philadelphians said it was all Benjamin Franklin's doings.

"Our Mr. Ben has saved the country! He has retrieved us from the brink of war!"

6

●●●●●●

Turmoil in Boston

Many Americans felt that the Stamp Act's repeal ended a long and bitter altercation with England, a tussle they had won. From now on the sailing would be smoother.

But Samuel Adams of Boston was unconvinced, cynical.

Adams and his associates frequented the Salutation Tavern in Ship Street. The Salutation was ancient, dingy, ramshackle, but cozy. Behind the public rooms was a smaller, private chamber, the meeting-place for Boston's North Caucus. There were three caucuses in the town, they were political clubs. Adams belonged to them all, but he was most often to be found at the Salutation, with his cousin John, Dr. Joseph Warren, the scholarly James Otis, Paul Revere and other Sons of Liberty.

Over bowls of spicy eggnog or brandy flip, smoking their white-stemmed clay pipes, the men sat and talked. Adams took little part in the conversation, but he listened acutely, his eyes bright, his palsied head nodding.

The Stamp Act was dead. But would the King give in so tamely? No! thought Adams. The King was merely having a breathing-spell, he would move again.

"For there'll always be a next move," Sam Adams said to

himself. "Always something, until we finally throw off the yoke of monarchy. And God speed that day!"

Then in 1767, Sir Charles Townshend, England's chancellor of the exchequer, secured the passage by Parliament of several bills that afterward were known by his name: the Townshend Acts.

One of these bills taxed the colonists for all importations of wine, oil, paper, glass, painter's colors, and tea. A second established boards of customs commissioners in the colonies to see that the customs regulations were strictly observed. A third provided that England was to pay the salaries of the judges and governors in the royal provinces, thus making these officials responsible only to the Crown and implying that only if they obeyed the Crown would they draw a salary. Another enactment decreed that Americans arrested for violation of revenue laws would be tried in admiralty courts, without juries.

At nearly the same time, Parliament suspended the functions of the New York legislature, because it had not voted funds for the upkeep of British regiments stationed in the colony.

Americans were shocked by the Townshend Acts, by Parliament's audacity in doing away with a colonial governing body on a pretext so feeble—or on any pretext.

One by one, their precious rights were being taken away.

In London, George III was also thinking about rights, his own, which he knew to be divine, coming straight from heaven.

It is in the very nature of things, thought George III, that subjects cannot dictate to a king, telling him what he must or must not do, which laws they will accept and which reject. The king who permits such insolence ceases to be a king, and is as nothing. Disobedience in a kingdom is like a stick of dynamite planted in the foundations of a noble building; it must be rooted out, for if it is ignited the whole structure will totter and crash.

George III was sure that in his every deed and proclamation he was motivated solely by his duty to England.

The Townshend Acts bore most severely on the northern colonies, and the first of the new customs commissions settled in at Boston.

"Ah, Boston!" said one of the commissioners. "If there's to be a fuss, it'll be here."

And so it was, a fuss soon occurring and centering about Samuel Adams's friend, John Hancock.

In 1768, John Hancock was thirty-one, tall and exceedingly slender, thin-faced, with a high forehead and a jutting chin. He had inherited his vast fortune from his uncle, Thomas Hancock. He lived in the family home on Beacon Hill where his Aunt Lydia, Thomas's elderly widow, was still the housekeeper and overseer of the servants. John's health was not robust; he was nervous and plagued by headaches; his adoring Aunt Lydia worried constantly about him. But like many persons afflicted with nervousness, he was vivacious and nimble as a squirrel.

"No grass ever grows under John's feet," said Aunt Lydia.

In attire he was very fastidious, a fashion plate; he set the styles for Boston dandies. His brocaded dressing gowns, purple topcoats, lavender jackets and velvet breeches of a pale lilac were sedulously copied. He wore jeweled buttons and frills of lace not only on his cuffs, but cascading down his shirt front. His wigs were curled to perfection.

He was conceited, touchy, petulant, but also open-handed and lavishly charitable. He had given the town a fire engine; he gave the library of Harvard College, his alma mater, a splendid collection of books; to churches he gave bells, pews and communion tables.

For a while he had been an officer in the Massachusetts militia; he still liked to call himself Colonel Hancock. But the paupers of Boston had another complimentary title for him.

He was very good to the paupers; they never had to ask twice for his favors. He let them cut wood from his forests. He fed and clothed scores of them. Sometimes he was host for great feasts on Boston Common, with oxen roasting in the charcoal pit, ale by the tubful, rum flowing like water. When he rode out in his shiny chaise, the horses prancing, harness jingling, his humble friends ran before him, shouting that he was their darling, their patron, squire—king!

King Hancock! The nickname tickled his vanity.

But for all his foppishness, affectations and love of display, John Hancock was a man of strong character. He had been attracted by Samuel Adams, and converted to his teachings. Hancock's belief in the colonists' cause was as sincere as Sam Adams's; but he did not believe, as Adams seemed to, that any means, whether fair or foul, were justified in attaining American independence. He had the rich man's regard for property; he winced at the destruction of anybody's property.

When Thomas Hutchinson's house was ravaged, Hancock had said: "Opposition to the Stamp Act is commendable. But I abhor the injury done to the lieutenant-governor and would go to great lengths to repair his loss."

In business, Hancock was shrewd. The heritage from his Uncle Thomas was extensive and varied. He employed a large staff of clerks, agents and accountants. He owned a book bindery, shops and warehouses, and dealt in innumerable and diverse stocks: stationery and lumber, whale oil and whalebone, codfish, cutlery, tea, dress goods, ribbons and fans, blankets, hourglasses and swords. In fact Bostonians could buy almost anything under the sun in John Hancock's stores.

He dabbled in real estate, too, buying and selling town lots, farms and timber tracts, transactions always profitable to him. But his biggest investment was in importing. In 1768, he owned three vessels and had an interest in twenty more, all of them fetching and carrying valuable cargoes across the Atlantic.

And sometimes, as his Uncle Thomas had done in the past, John Hancock indulged in smuggling.

"Dear John, what with this and that, he has scant leisure," Aunt Lydia once remarked to a lady drinking tea with her in the Beacon Hill parlor.

"No wonder!" said the visiting lady.

The customs officials knew that John Hancock had said he would brook no interference with his shipping. They thought this was an indication that he intended to evade the lawful import duties, and when his brigantine, the *Lydia,* arrived at his wharf one April day in 1768, they ordered two tidesmen, Owen Richards and Robert Jackson, to inspect its cargo.

"Oh, no!" said Captain Scott of the *Lydia* to the tidesmen as they came on deck. "You'll do no inspecting. Mr. Hancock won't have it."

"We've got our orders," Richards said.

Captain Scott then sent a sailor to Hancock's house. Hancock hurried to the wharf, so angry, his voice so loud, that the tidesmen were intimidated.

But that night Richards returned and crept stealthily down into the ship's hold, unaware that he had been seen by a fisherman on the wharf. The fisherman, a friend of Hancock's, ran to Beacon Hill, where Hancock was eating a late supper.

Hancock was finicky about his food, he had a gourmet's

appetite and disliked being disturbed at his meals. But he rose instantly from the table.

"Get my hat, Cato," he said to his Negro butler, "and come along with us."

On the way to the wharf with Cato and the fisherman, he was joined by eight more of his friends. Briskly boarding the *Lydia*, he rousted out Captain Scott, the mate and the boatswain from their berths, informed them of the intruder and told them to hustle him up on deck.

"Now, tidesman," Hancock said when Richards, rather the worse for bruises and lumps, was hauled before him, "you may search every inch of the brigantine—*except* the hold. You'll not tamper with my cargo. Well, get started! My friends are here to see that you make a good job of it."

Richards stared at Mr. Hancock's friends. Sons of Liberty, weren't they? Sons of Perdition, you'd best call 'em! Richards had heard stories aplenty about these ruffians. Get sassy with 'em and they hang you in effigy, break your windows and your bones, tar and feather you! Oh, yes, there were customs men the Sons had tarred and feathered, and a nasty trick it was, enough to curdle your blood!

Richards said he wouldn't search the *Lydia*, after all.

Somehow, though it was eleven o'clock, a crowd had massed on the wharf. Richard's eye was blacked, the sleeves ripped from his coat and his toes tramped on, but he congratulated himself for getting out with his skin in one piece.

The crowd escorted Hancock back to Beacon Hill.

"I thank you, boys, but entreat you not to wake the town," he said. "Good night, sweet dreams!"

The customs commissioners had not finished with John Hancock. In May his sloop, the *Liberty*, docked at his wharf. James Marshall, the *Liberty's* captain filed a statement that the cargo consisted of twenty-five casks of wine from Madeira.

"A small consignment," the commissioners said. "Suspiciously small. It must be checked."

This time a tidesman named Kirk was the inspector. When he stepped aboard the sloop, Captain Marshall disposed of him by the simple expedient of pushing him into the cabin and nailing up the door. Crouched there, Kirk could hear the creak of the hoisting apparatus unloading the wine casks. Twenty-five casks? A hundred, at least! thought Kirk.

At midnight, Marshall opened the cabin door. "If you're not an idiot, you'll keep your mouth shut, tidesman," he said.

Kirk was not an idiot; for a month he kept his mouth shut. Then, plucking up his courage, he told the commissioners about his misadventure. The *Romney*, a fifty-gun British frigate, had just then come to anchor in Boston harbor. On orders from the commissioners, sailors from the *Romney* cut the *Liberty* from her moorings, towed her under the frigate's guns and chained her tight.

Again John Hancock's friends, and even more of them, were on the water front. They hurled stones, bricks and mud at the British sailors and at the commissioners. They lifted a boat belonging to the chief customs collector, took it to the Common and burned it. The frightened commissioners, with their families, fled to Fort William on Castle Island, where Governor Sir Francis Bernard was already hiding.

The King's advocate in London notified the attorney general of Massachusetts that John Hancock had flouted the law and insulted the King. Hancock was arrested, charged with tax evasion and told that he must pay a fine of £100,000. Hancock retorted that no law had been violated. He demanded that his sloop be given back to him.

Hancock was tried in 1769. John Adams was his lawyer. For three months the trial lagged on. The tidesman Kirk was a weak and stammering witness, and there seemed to be no one else to testify. At last the attorney general dropped the case for lack of evidence.

Hancock's trial did not hurt his popularity with his fellow citizens; if anything, he was even more admired. He never got the *Liberty* back, nor did he admit that he was, or ever had been, a smuggler.

At about the time of John Hancock's arrest, the Crown officials in Boston advised Parliament that the town had been taken over by a "trained mob" which they were unable to subdue. Parliament had then ordered General Thomas Gage, commander-in-chief of the British army in America, to transfer two regiments of His Majesty's infantry and a detachment of artillery from Halifax to Boston, where the troops would serve as a police force.

Seven British battleships brought the soldiers, and the ships anchored offshore. The soldiers disembarked, and in columns-of-four marched up the Long Wharf, drums beating, fifes squealing. It was Saturday, October 1, 1768, and all Boston was out to see the procession, but the packed streets were strangely quiet.

Paul Revere walked from his shop on Clark's Wharf into King Street. He stood at a corner beside William Dawes, a young member of Samuel Adams's political club. Dawes usually had a cheerful, good-humored countenance, but his mouth was now twisted in a grimace.

"A police force, eh?" he said. "We've never had a police force, so they're giving us one. Very nice."

"That's Gage," Revere said. "The officer with the most gold braid on his bonnet."

"Ah? Neat as wax, ain't he? Well, they all are. All prunes and prisms. I hate 'em."

"Gage will stay until the troops are installed," Revere said. "Then he'll go on to New York."

"Leaving his boys—for us to feed and house. And maybe we won't. No telling! Revere, did you know we've got a *trained* mob in Boston?"

Revere smiled. "I've never thought of it as that."

"I'll bet the redcoats'll be sorry they've come," Dawes said.

Nearby, Samuel Adams also watched the soldiers as they marched. He did not hate them. His hatred was never for men, but for ideas, concepts, which he felt were contrary to truth, contemptible. The concept of sovereignty, that was false, and there must be no compromising with it, not even temporarily.

Adams looked at the people around him. They seemed stunned, their faces were blank, expressionless; he wished that he could read their thoughts. Those thoughts wouldn't invariably coincide with his. Oh, no! Boston had its loyalists, not so many as some towns, but still too many. Such people were now spoken of as Tories, because of their sympathy with the Tory party in England, the party that maintained the supremacy of the Crown over the innate rights of human beings.

To Samuel Adams, the Tories in America seemed more evil than the English Tories, more treacherous. They wore no badge or label, you didn't know who they were, or where, couldn't put your finger on them. They were the unidentified enemy, wolves in sheep's clothing, mingling with the flock. Of course, in time they would reveal themselves. But even then, Adams would not hate them; he would pity them for their insensibility, their blindness.

Turning from the procession, he walked homeward. His house in Purchase Street, a dreary section of Boston, was drab and dilapidated, almost tumbling about his ears. Well, what was a house? The neighbors whispered that if it weren't for Mr. John Hancock's charity, the family of Sam Adams would often go hungry. And what of that? Wasn't Hancock his friend? Is an exchange of gifts necessary between friends? If so, he had presented Hancock with something, too—the priceless something he offered all his friends—a doctrine, a purpose, a realization of the eternal and undaunted spirit of man.

At his gate, he was greeted by an acquaintance.

"Good day, Mr. Adams. You saw the British regulars? And what d'you think, sir, of their coming here?"

Rather as William Dawes had done, Adams said: "I think they may rue it. I think they may be very unhappy in Boston."

7

●●●●●●

Violence by Moonlight

Americans viewed the installing of a military "police force" in Boston as one more infringement of their rights. And in 1769, they had still another for the ever-growing list.

Long ago, in the sixteenth century, when England was a small ocean-girded kingdom, with no colonies anywhere, Parliament had passed a law authorizing the trial, conviction and punishment in England of English subjects accused of crimes committed outside of the British Isles. The law was so old that it was virtually forgotten. Now Parliament and George III talked of reviving it. Thus, colonists charged with treason might be haled to England for trial in an English court.

Americans shuddered at the prospect. If the law should be made operative again, it would mean that on accusation alone, whether valid or trumped-up, they could be taken from their homes to have their innocence or guilt determined in a land which they now felt was hostile to them. The King would see any balking of his imperious will as treason, a crime for which the penalty was death. Who but the deluded could believe that such trials would be fair and unprejudiced?

75

In May, in the Virginia House of Burgesses, George Washington strenuously protested against a law so vicious in its possibilities—so much worse than the Stamp Act, the Townshend Acts. Washington had written a paper, which he read to the burgesses. Freedom, he said, must be defended!

"No man should hesitate a moment to use arms in defence of so valuable a blessing."

Arms? The burgesses were somewhat startled. This was not Patrick Henry, shaking the rafters with emotional oratory. It wasn't Samuel Adams, the Massachusetts extremist. No, it was Washington, sane, cool and prudent always, the one American most experienced in the use of arms, the one best qualified to know what such usage entailed.

As the burgesses reflected, George Mason, a member from Fairfax County, read a new series of Virginia Resolves that he himself had framed.

Mason was a man of integrity, a close friend of Washington's; the two often rode and hunted together. Mason's ancestors for generations had been Virginia aristocrats and planters. He lived at Gunston Hall, an estate of great beauty and elegance.

Mason's Resolves enumerated all the grievances the colonists had suffered, asked that they be corrected, and stated that "all trials for any crime whatsoever" should be held within the colony where the crime was alleged to have been committed.

The burgesses, having heard the new Resolves, voted unanimously to adopt them, and the speaker of the House was instructed to send copies to the other colonies, seeking their concurrence. A formal letter to the King, written by Patrick Henry and Richard Henry Lee, was then adopted.

And just at this point, as the enthusiasm of the meeting soared, Virginia's royal governor, the Baron de Botetourt, stalked into the capitol. The burgesses might resolve to their heart's content; the governor could dissolve—and did.

"The session of this legislative body is dissolved," announced de Botetourt. "Yes, gentlemen, *dissolved*."

Turned out into the street, as if they were a public nuisance, the burgesses went to the Raleigh Tavern, reconvened at once and speedily voted through a non-importation agreement, by which they bound themselves neither to use nor to import, henceforth, any goods on which Parliament had levied a tax. Among the signatures affixed to the document was that of Thomas Jefferson, a newcomer to Virginia politics.

Thomas Jefferson was then twenty-six, a native of Albemarle County, a graduate of William and Mary College. For five years he had studied law with George Wythe, the dean of the Virginia bar, and had served as a justice of the peace, until his election as a burgess.

Jefferson was very tall, broad-shouldered, slim-waisted, sinewy. His hair was sandy, faintly red, his complexion ruddy, his eyes gray. He was considered to be more charming than handsome. He was singularly amiable and unpretentious; his habits were simple. He loved music and outdoor sports and was an expert horseman. His interests and talents rivaled those of Benjamin Franklin, and like Franklin, he was an inventive genius.

In 1769, Thomas Jefferson was an attractive and finely educated young man, as yet inconspicuous, but destined to rise rapidly to fame and to be at last immortalized in his country's history.

Virginia's non-importation agreement drew promises of the same sort from the other colonies, and soon English merchants engaged in colonial trade were feeling the pinch of a greatly reduced market for their wares. This was exactly what the colonists had hoped for.

"The merchants have influence in Parliament," they said, "and may exert it."

Hopefully they waited, and by the year's end were gratified to learn that the merchants had begged for repeal of the Townshend Acts.

The members of Parliament were in a quandary, for the merchants' influence was not a thing to be discounted. And, really, the Townshend Acts had been almost a complete failure—the revenue brought into the exchequer scarcely covered the expense of collecting it. So, in January, 1770, the Acts were repealed.

But there would still be a tax on tea. This tax was retained at the King's insistence. Though it was trifling, the tea tax was a symbol by which the colonies acknowledged George III as their master.

The King held on tenaciously to the tea tax, as a drowning man clutches for a straw.

In the East, the Sons of Liberty had been busy with the brand of mischief at which they excelled. In New York, they clashed with British troops, who had cut down their liberty pole. The civilians recaptured the pole and erected it again. A few skulls were cracked in the affray, a few noses bloodied and a dozen people jailed, but there were no fatalities.

In Boston, the story was different and more somber.

Bostonians had been shocked by the arrival of the British regiments. Now they were consumed with the wish for revenge. Of course, the King was the object of this wish, but he was in London, not to be reached. His soldiers, who were here, must answer for his sins!

The soldiers had been told that they would have adequate living quarters in Boston. The townsfolk had no intention of furnishing such accommodations, and in fact couldn't have done so—with the influx of more than a thousand despised interlopers, Boston was bursting at the seams. Until barracks were built for the British officers, the men had to camp wherever they found room—in tents on the Common, in cellars and garrets, distilleries and stables, in the corridors of the State House and Faneuil Hall.

Scattered as the men were, the officers could not supervise them properly. Discipline was lax, and soldiers wandered idly about the town, squabbling, gambling, drinking and brawling. And as foreseen by William Dawes and Samuel Adams, and probably many others, they were not happy. In the first two weeks of their American sojourn, thirty of them deserted. In the following months there were more deserters, some of whom were caught and executed, shot down by firing squads in full sight of their comrades.

From the beginning, the redcoats were a target for the Boston rowdies, whose incessant persecution was unplanned but none the less vigorous. "Lobsters" they were called—"*Lobsters!*" They were heckled and badgered, jeered at and jolted, and could not return the compliments except on the sly, when their officers weren't looking.

March 5, 1770, was a day of very cold weather in Boston. Snow fell in the morning and afternoon, but at evening the sky cleared and at night the moon shone. John Goldsmith, a British captain, walked in the bright moonlight from his barracks in Brattle Street to have a word with the guards posted around the corner in King Street.

Captain Goldsmith was a good enough officer, but he was in debt to tradesmen of the town, particularly to Monsieur Piemont, a French barber and wigmaker. As Goldsmith entered King Street, a ragged boy pounced at him, tugged at his sleeve and with a stream of profanity demanded the money owed to Monsieur Piemont.

Goldsmith recognized the boy as the wigmaker's apprentice, and he pushed him aside and walked on. But a sentry named Hugh Montgomery, on guard at the Customs House, heard the outcry. Running from his box, Montgomery grabbed the boy and slapped his face.

"Murder!" the boy screamed and slumped to the ground. *"Murder!"*

Instantly people came surging into King Street, all of them shouting that a sentry had assaulted and murdered a child. The wigmaker's apprentice got up and darted away, but the crowd milled frantically about in the square in front of the State House, advanced upon Montgomery and continued to shout, "Murder, murder!"

Then, abruptly, the bell in the steeple of Old South Church tolled, and went on tolling. More people came scrambling out of their houses into the square, some carrying buckets of water, shrieking that the town was afire. Hurrying up from the wharfs came a riffraff gang of cursing, swaggering sailors.

Montgomery, surrounded, was pale with terror and rage. The day had been a hard one for him; he had been pelted with snowballs, oyster shells, chunks of ice, and for hours had been on solitary duty, a stint that every sentry dreaded because of the rowdies' taunts and torment. Montgomery was hungry and cold, and the faces staring at him were flushed with fury.

"Come near me and I'll blow your brains out!" Montgomery threatened.

The reply was a roar: "Shoot and be damned!"

As Montgomery loaded his musket, a Bostonian named Crispus Attucks leaped toward him, brandishing a cordwood club. Crispus Attucks was a giant of a man, a mulatto, part white, part Negro and Indian.

"Lobster!" Attucks yelled, and poked his club into Montgomery's ribs. "Lobster, I'll have one o' your claws!'

The sailors laughed raucously at this sally, and there were

yells of "Kill the lobster! Kill him!" Desperately, Montgomery screamed, "Main guard, turn out! *Main guard!*"

From King Street, the main guard led by Captain John Preston, officer of the day, trotted at double-time. Captain Preston shouted, "Prime and load!" but he thrust himself between his men and the crowd, arms outstretched, as if to prevent an onslaught.

There was an eerie pause, in which the only noise was the rattle of ramrods as the soldiers loaded their guns. Then Attucks lifted his club, struck at Preston, missed, and instead knocked down Montgomery, and fell on top of him. Attucks snatched at Montgomery's gun. They clinched and rolled struggling in the snow. Wrenching the gun from Attucks's grasp, Montgomery staggered to his feet just as a command rang out: *"Fire!"*

Montgomery fired two bullets through Attucks's chest. The huge mulatto dropped, dead as a stone. Howling, maddened, the crowd rushed toward the guards. "Fire away, you damned lobster-backs!"

A barrage of shots sounded, more civilians keeled over, the snow was stained with blood.

Now alarm drums were thumping, soldiers running from every section of the town, muskets ready, bayonets glittering in the moonlight. Somebody, Captain Preston perhaps, cried: "Hutchinson! Fetch Hutchinson!" Several troopers scurried off in search of the lieutenant governor.

Since Sir Francis Bernard's exit, Thomas Hutchinson had been the chief magistrate of Massachusetts. Never a coward, he came immediately to the square, shouldered through the seething, clamorous press, entered the State House and appeared on the east balcony.

He looked down. At one side of the street were the soldiers, standing or kneeling, guns leveled. Across from them were the civilians, held at bay, cringing yet still defiant. Again there was a brief silence.

"Go to your homes!" Hutchinson said. "Let the law settle this thing. Let the law have its course. I myself will live and die by the law. Let you also keep to this principle. Blood has been shed, awful work done this night. Go home! Tomorrow there will be an inquiry."

As the people saw Hutchinson on the balcony above them, his figure plainly silhouetted by the lamplit windows, as they listened to him, they seemed to forget that he was a Tory, a loyal servant of the King. Once they had respected him— they respected him now. Slowly they dispersed.

The officers then marched the soldiers back to quarters, leaving a guard of a hundred men to patrol King Street, the square and the docks.

Four citizens of Boston had been killed: Crispus Attucks, Samuel Gray, Samuel Maverick, James Caldwell. A fifth, Patrick Carr, would die of his wounds. Six more were wounded, though not seriously.

Before sunrise next morning Captain Preston, Hugh Montgomery and the seven men of the main guard were arrested for murder. They would be tried, they must have lawyers to plead for them.

Where were the lawyers to attempt such a task?

8

●●●●●●

Redcoats on Trial

On that wild night of March 5, John Adams had attended
a political meeting in south Boston. When the church bell
started to ring, the streets resounded with angry voices,
Adams guessed that the mob was out again. At once, thinking of his family, he hastened to his small house in Cold
Lane. He had a wife whom he dearly loved, a little daughter
named Abigail, for her mother, and a two-year-old son, John
Quincy Adams. No harm must befall them! John Adams believed implicitly in liberty, but he would define it for himself.
Many Americans, he thought, were now confusing liberty
with license—and a mob is as mindless, and often as cruel, as
a rabid animal.

Adams was thirty-four, short and stout, strong-willed. He
had been born on his father's farm near Braintree. After
graduation from Harvard College, he had taught school in
Worcester, then had studied law. He was intelligent, industrious, incorruptible, and despite a manner which was
brusque and at times even unpleasant, he had built up a good
practice in Boston.

When he went to his office on Tuesday morning, Adams
saw that with daylight, the town's excitement had re-

awakened. There were people clustered on every street corner, and throngs seemed to be coming in from the country: men and boys carrying rakes, pitchforks, squirrel guns. The British sentries were at their posts. No one molested them, but they looked morose, uneasy.

At his office, Adams soon had a caller—a Mr. Forester who bore in Boston the peculiar nickname of the Irish Infant. Mr. Forester was a Tory and a friend of the young British officers. He seemed much distressed now: when Adams asked him to be seated, he sank into a chair, wiped his brow with his handkerchief and wept.

"Mr. Adams," he said, "I've been to the jail, talking with Captain Preston. If you could see Preston, so bruised and battered! He tells me he didn't order the guards to fire. When those scoundrels sprang on him, he hit at them—with his fists. But he was unarmed, had no weapon of any kind. He had run from his barracks without gun or sword. And all the while he was shouting, 'Don't fire!' But the din was so great he couldn't be heard. Mr. Adams, were you in King Street last night?"

"No," Adams said.

"Well, I assure you, sir, that Captain Preston is not prevaricating, he would not lie—"

"Mr. Forester," interrupted Adams, "why are you here?"

"To ask your help," Forester said. "Preston must have a lawyer and can't get one. Without a lawyer to plead for him, he'll be condemned—executed. Naturally, he thought first of the loyalist attorneys in Boston; there are some. I have been to them, but they will not take the case. They won't risk it. They fear the Sons of Liberty. . . . Mr. Adams, do you know Robert Auchmuty, the admiralty judge?"

"Yes, I know Mr. Auchmuty. Pray compose yourself, Mr. Forester."

Forester nodded and mopped his tears. "Well, sir, Mr.

Auchmuty is braver than the rest of the Tory lawyers. He said that if I could get you to work with him, he would represent Preston. You belong to the *people's* faction, Mr. Adams. You're known as a patriot."

Adams smiled mirthlessly. "I daresay I am."

"From Mr. Auchmuty's I went to see Mr. Josiah Quincy Jr. He also is of the people's faction, and a relative of yours—"

"Of my wife's, a distant relative."

Forester continued, "Josiah Quincy told me the same: he is willing to take the case, if you'll conduct it. Sir, you must! You have a splendid reputation; you were John Hancock's attorney in the *Liberty* matter. Hancock was fairly tried. Preston's trial will not be fair—unless you plead for him. The town is against him, crying for his blood. And he is innocent!"

Adams gestured impatiently. "That must be ascertained by the evidence."

"Perjured evidence! All perjured!"

As Forester paused, Adams was thinking hard. Outside, there were Indian yells, shrill whistling. Was it the mob? More trouble?

Adams thought of the Sons of Liberty, of whom he was a patron and partisan, and he thought of his political clubs and caucuses. If he should take Preston's case, many of his associates would never understand it. A risk? Yes, indeed, a grave risk! John Adams's reputation—his splendid reputation—would be at stake, and much else too, friendships that meant a great deal to him, that might not survive such a test.

And it was not to be doubted that Boston would cry for Preston's blood. Already the patriot folk thirsted for vengeance, an eye for an eye, a tooth for a tooth. Preston, as a British soldier, was an enemy. The lawyer who defended him would have all the town's hatred to fight.

But suppose Preston was the truthful man Forester believed him to be? Perhaps he hadn't given the command to fire last night—had instead shouted, *"Don't fire!"* and his voice was drowned in the uproar. It was entirely possible. And even your bitterest enemy deserves justice. How can a man ask justice for himself if he withholds it from others?

"Mr. Forester," Adams said.

"Yes, sir?"

"If Captain Preston feels he cannot get a fair trial without my help, then he shall have it."

Forester jumped from his chair, as though to embrace Adams. "Oh, sir, my infinite thanks!"

Never demonstrative, Adams frowned a little and opened the office door. "I bid you good day now," he said crisply.

As Forester descended the steps to the street, he passed Benjamin Edes, who had stopped on the pavement. Edes was the editor of the *Boston Gazette*, a fiercely anti-Tory newspaper. Edes glanced at Forester, then up at Adams in the doorway.

"The Irish Infant!" Edes exclaimed. "What's he want of you, John?"

"Ben Edes," Adams said, "you may inform anyone who is interested that I'm going to represent Captain Preston when he is tried for murder."

Edes gasped. "Oh, no!"

"Yes, and I shall also defend the eight British regulars. Good day to you, Ben."

Turning, John Adams closed his door and went back to his desk.

At eleven o'clock that morning, more than a thousand Bostonians met in Faneuil Hall to demand the removal of the British regiments from the town. John Adams's cousin Samuel presided at the meeting. Sam Adams said that a message had been sent earlier to Lieutenant Governor Hutchinson. "But as yet," he said, "Mr. Hutchinson has not deigned to respond."

A committee of fifteen was then selected to go to the State House, where Hutchinson and other Crown officials were consulting. The committee was to tell the lieutenant governor that the soldiers must be withdrawn immediately or Boston would not answer for the consequences.

Headed by Adams, the committee left, and at three in the afternoon returned. Hutchinson had said that he had not the power to issue orders to the King's troops; but when Adams disputed this, he had hedged a bit and said he might arrange to have one of the two regiments transferred to Castle Island in the harbor.

"One regiment!" said Samuel Adams, from the platform in Faneuil Hall. "My friends, it must be *both regiments or none!*"

"Ay, ay!" the audience cried. "*Both regiments or none!*"

"This is your decision?"

"Ay, ay, Sam!"

"Very well," he said. "I shall convey it to the magistrates."

Through softly falling snow, the committee trudged again to the State House. The King's men, in powdered wigs and scarlet cloaks, sat at a table in an upper chamber. They looked grand but somewhat gloomy. As always, Samuel Adams was shabby and ill-groomed, his coat wrinkled, his gray hair straggling on his collar.

"Mr. Hutchinson," Adams said, pointing a palsied finger. "Mr. Hutchinson, if you can remove one regiment, you can remove two. And so it must be. The people have spoken. Fifteen thousand Massachusetts men are waiting. They will not wait much longer. They will rise!"

The Crown officials whispered among themselves. A

British officer got up. This was Colonel Dalrymple, the commander of all the British troops in Boston. He addressed the lieutenant governor.

"Sir, I think it would be advisable to send both regiments to Castle Island. The civilians are out in vast crowds and some of them are armed."

Hutchinson rubbed his chin and sighed bleakly. "Mr. Adams," he said, "tell the people that we grant their petition. But a little time will be needed for the transfer."

Adams bowed. "I will tell them."

Almost at once, the event of March 5, 1770, was referred to as a massacre—the Boston Massacre. Who coined the phrase? Was it Samuel Adams or Paul Revere?

Adams was distrustful of how Thomas Hutchinson or Colonel Dalrymple might report the night's happenings to King George and Parliament. He wrote his own report: *A Short Narrative of the Horrid Massacre in Boston . . . with some observations on the state of things prior to that catastrophe.*

The "short narrative" was thirty-two pages of closely written foolscap. He got it off to England by the first boat, and broadcast copies of it through the colonies.

The massacre *was* a catastrophe. Of course, it was. And yet, Adams thought, it was, in its way, a godsend. It had fanned a flame, the flame of rebellion that must not be allowed to flicker out!

Paul Revere was not only a silversmith, he was also a jeweler, a printer, an engraver, a dentist who made beautiful false teeth, and something of an artist. In his fascinating shop on Clark's Wharf, Revere sketched a pen-and-ink diagram of the State House square, showing the buildings and the exact positions of the soldiers and their victims when the rioting there had been at its height. The diagram, he thought, might be useful in the trial of the soldiers.

Then, stirred by patriotism and quick to discern a business opportunity, he made a colored engraving which he printed and, as he said, sold "like hot cakes."

The engraving was striking, but more fanciful than accurate. The townsfolk were portrayed as a small, meek-looking group. There was no snow, and the moon was a crescent faintly etched in a blue-washed sky. The soldiers, vivid in black hats and red uniforms, had symmetrical clouds of brown smoke ballooning from their guns. Behind them, Captain Preston waved a sword, plainly urging them to shoot. And in the foreground, the very center of the picture, was a black-and-white dog, quite calm in the midst of turmoil.

THE BLOODY MASSACRE: so Paul Revere entitled his engraving, in big type, and beneath were verses describing it.

The four Bostonians who had been killed, the "martyrs" as they now were called, were buried on Thursday, March 8. It was a day of sorrow, crepe streamers, funeral wreaths. Hundreds of black-clad mourners followed the four hearses and watched as the coffins were lowered into the earth. Patrick Carr, the fifth victim, was still alive, conscious, but soon to die.

March 27, though, was a day of contrast. Colonel Dalrymple marched His Majesty's troops down the Long Wharf and embarked them for Castle Island. The sun shone, the streets were lined with jubilant spectators. The Sons of Liberty were there to escort the soldiers. The bully Mackintosh brought his clique. Packs of small boys skittered about, shrieking, "*Lobsters! Hup-hup! Who buys lobsters?*"

As Bostonians laughed, sang and clapped hands for joy, the Britishers paced stolidly, stiffly—and probably nearer happiness than they had been in months. They had not liked the town. It was a lunatic asylum!

John Adams requested and obtained a postponement of the trials. He had spent long hours talking with Preston and the guards, and he believed that the statutory charge against them would not hold water. But public sentiment was to be reckoned with.

"Our clients are now so hated that the chance of getting an unprejudiced judgment would be slight," he said to his colleagues, Robert Auchmuty and Josiah Quincy. "I want the case to be decided by *law*, not by emotions. It will be much to the clients' advantage to delay until this excitement has somewhat abated—for, in the best of circumstances, our work will be uphill all the way."

And, as he had expected, he was encountering censure himself. To many of his friends, it seemed very odd that John Adams, an avowed patriot, should defend the King's minions, the contemptible creatures of royalty—and criminals at that!

"Odd?" said the Boston hoodlums. "It's *wrong*. We'll fix 'im!"

Never mind, Adams thought, as stones were thrown through his windows and anonymous letters reviled him. "Never mind," he said to his wife. "I'm at peace with my conscience."

Captain Preston was tried in October, in a thronged and tense courtroom. All eyes were on John Adams, cool and austere in his barrister's gray wig, the sober black gown with its starched white bib. He told himself that he *must* win this case. It was imperative to win it, not only for Preston's sake, not only for the sake of abstract justice, but because England, Europe, all the world would note the outcome. By winning this case, he would be dignifying the American colonies, their ideals and aspirations. It must never be said that Americans were an inferior people, dominated by irresponsible mobs, with no understanding of human rights.

Many witnesses testified. Those for the prosecution said that the British soldiers, always ferocious as wolves, had rushed snarling at civilians on the night in question. Had they been teased a little, called insulting names? Yes, but the crowd in the square was unarmed. Captain Preston, ordering the sentries to fire, had been bound to know that the result would be wholesale murder—as it certainly was! Murder and nothing less!

Witnesses for the defense contradicted such testimony. The civilians, they said, had instigated the riot.

The attorneys argued. Preston's attorneys, led by Adams, contended that the captain had done nothing beyond the performance of his duty. Summoned to quell the pandemonium, he had gone into it without weapons, but when attacked by persons in the crowd, he had exchanged blows with them. A soldier on duty has the right to do so—as has any and every man. Name calling is one thing. But to prod a man with a stick, to take him by the hair, the ears or nose, to knock him down, kick him, is something else. This is physical violence, and the law does not oblige a man to bear it. Lay hands on a man and he is within his legal rights to lay hands on *you!*

A voice had been heard to cry, *Fire!* But whose voice? Captain Preston denied that it was his. Where was the witness who would swear—on the Holy Bible!—that Preston had uttered the command? If Preston was a murderer, who could say which of the four dead Bostonians he had murdered?

The trial lasted six days. Then the jury rendered its verdict: not guilty.

Adams was glad, but there was still the trial of the eight guards to prepare for.

The second trial was held in November. Again the courtroom was full. The soldiers looked thin and pallid after their months of imprisonment. They were frightened and sat with bowed heads.

Josiah Quincy was young, frail in health, but an efficient lawyer and good speaker. The jury listened carefully to his examination of the witnesses and his polished argument. When Adams spoke, it was without flourishes or fine language; as usual, he was blunt and candid.

He quoted the English statute: that a party of soldiers, legally assembled and sent by their officers to the relief of other soldiers, may defend themselves, even to the death of those who would obstruct them. The soldiers here on trial had been legally assembled, he said, whereas the civilians were an illegal and dangerous gathering, a mob. The sentry, Hugh Montgomery, and the men of the main guard had really believed their lives were endangered. They were eight against two hundred or more. They were hemmed in—and somebody had cried, *Fire!*

In this case, Adams and Josiah Quincy were aided by the testimony of Dr. Jeffries, the Boston surgeon who had attended Patrick Carr when Carr was dying.

On his deathbed, Carr had said to Dr. Jeffries: "The soldiers were much abused. I believe they fired in self-defense. I believe that if they had not done so, they would all have been killed. I am dying, but I have malice toward no one."

On December 5, the jury found six of the accused men not guilty. Hugh Montgomery and one other, Matthew Killroy, were found guilty of manslaughter.

John Adams asked the judges for benefit of clergy for these two. Benefit of clergy was an old English law whereby the guilty person could be branded on the thumb and then discharged. The judges granted Adams's request. Montgomery and Killroy stood up, stretched out their hands, and the white-hot iron was applied to their thumbs.

The trial was over. The courtroom emptied. The soldiers turned to John Adams, thanking him effusively.

"Don't thank me," he said sternly. "I was convinced of your innocence, according to the law. I wanted only justice and feel that I got it. Go to the wharf and get a boat for Castle Island. You will not be safe in Boston."

"But what about you, Mr. Adams?" they said. "Will you be safe?"

He drew himself up and frowned. "You have been acquitted by a jury of Americans, my countrymen. This is my home. I have nothing to fear in Boston."

9

●●●●●●

Rhode Island Incident

In the early months of 1771, the colonists felt that their relations with England were less strained. Radicals of Samuel Adams's stripe might continue to visualize complete independence, but most Americans wanted only the amount of self-government that would let them live on terms of dignity and peace with King and Parliament. They had been soothed by the repeal of the Townshend Acts; after the removal of the British troops from Boston, they were willing to believe that things had taken a turn for the better, the King was mellowing, Parliament coming around to a more rational view.

Of course, there was the tea tax to remind them that George III hadn't relinquished quite all his stubborn notions —a reminder as persistently annoying as a pebble in the shoe, but not really a hardship. Even with the tax, tea could be bought cheaply in America, at a lower price than English buyers paid. And it need not be bought at all. Many colonists had quit buying it. English exporters were finding, to their chagrin, that in colonial society, tea-drinking was going out of fashion.

This was almost a tranquil period in Boston. The mobs

were out only infrequently; their wrangling and scuffling was largely among themselves. The more respectable people of the town were talking about promoting the arts, agriculture, manufacturing and commerce in Massachusetts. John Hancock was engrossed in charitable enterprises. As Boston squire and philanthropist, Hancock had built a bandstand on the Common and hired musicians to give concerts there. He was improving and beautifying an area near his Beacon Hill mansion, making it a public park with graveled paths, flower beds and a fenced-in playground for children. He lamented the fact that the streets were so dark at night, and planned to purchase lamps for their proper illumination.

Sir Francis Bernard had gone back to England—without regret. "I had supposed my position would be delightful," said Sir Francis. "Like a country vacation! But, alas, it was not!" Thomas Hutchinson had been elevated to the place Bernard left; now Hutchinson was the colony's royal governor.

Thomas Hutchinson was anxious that his situation be clearly understood: he was unswervingly loyal to the King, everybody must know it. As he took his office, he told the Massachusetts legislators that at all times he would uphold the authority of the Crown and Parliament.

"Defiance of any sort cannot be pardoned," he said. "The one alternative to submission is rebellion. There is no middle ground."

To Samuel Adams, this statement of Hutchinson's seemed perfectly sensible—it was what Adams had been saying all along. There was no middle ground. Nor did Adams think for a minute that the King had mellowed, that Parliament was relenting.

In 1771, Adams was organizing local Committees of Correspondence in the Massachusetts towns and villages, contriving a network by which information could be spread to every corner of the colony, with express riders serving as private and confidential couriers.

"We must be equipped to communicate in times of stress," he said. "Nothing is more important than the means of communication."

He was pleased when Virginia and then Rhode Island, Connecticut, New Hampshire and South Carolina adopted his scheme. Soon all the colonies would be linked, so that news bulletins, letters, brochures and pamphlets could be rapidly circulated from one to the other.

"And *warnings*," Adams said to himself, "if the occasion should arise—as I think it may."

In March of 1772, the *Gaspee*, an English armed vessel commanded by Lieutenant Duddington of the royal navy, anchored in Boston harbor. The sight of a ship flying the King's colors was no novelty in these waters: a half-dozen of His Majesty's men-of-war were always there, snouting ugly guns toward the town. But the *Gaspee* was uniquely interesting to loungers on the wharves. Hadn't they seen her somewhere before?

"Why, she looks like John Hancock's *Liberty!*" they exclaimed. "By jinks, she *is* the *Liberty!* Yessir, she's Hancock's pretty sloop, the one they stole from him—and repainted and fixed up a bit!"

The *Gaspee* did not stay in the harbor. Lieutenant Duddington sailed for Narragansett Bay. It was said that smugglers were operating between Newport and Providence, and the Boston customs officials had sent Duddington to nab them.

The wharf loungers were horrified at this. "Hancock's sloop made into a revenue cutter? It's a blasted shame!"

In Narragansett Bay, Lieutenant Duddington was very busy. He hovered around Providence. Any boat setting out from that port was likely to be chased by the *Gaspee* and, if overtaken, searched thoroughly for smuggled goods. The Providence merchants were resentful; they said that Duddington had no legal warrants and was interfering with the free navigation of the bay. They went to Joseph Wanton, the governor of Rhode Island, and remonstrated.

Wanton, though a Tory and a royal magistrate, was a native Rhode Islander and popular in the colony. He notified Lieutenant Duddington that the illegal searching must be stopped. Duddington replied that he would do as he pleased, and the British admiralty would support him.

At noon on June 9, 1772, an American captain named Lindsey left Newport for Providence in his packet, the *Hannah*. Lindsey regularly made a round trip from New York to Providence, touching at Newport to unload or take on cargo. Every mile of the coast and bordering waters was as familiar to him as the palm of his own hand. The wind on this June day was strong from the south; he expected a speedy voyage in good weather.

He had not gone far when he saw that he was followed.

"The *Gaspee*, that pirate Duddington," Lindsey said to his mate.

"Reckon we're in for a chase?" the mate asked.

"Reckon so," said Lindsey. "Duddington's getting too big for his britches. We'll have a little fun with him, and show the Britishers a thing or two."

Namquit Point was a treacherous place in the approach to Providence. The point was a long sand bar extending out into the bay, deeply covered at flood tide, but a trap for inexperienced sailors when the tide ebbed and the water was shallow. Captain Lindsey knew all about Namquit. Reaching it at ebb tide, he swung the *Hannah* well out to sea, away from the shoals. Gracefully doubling the point, he looked back—and saw, as he had hoped to see, that Duddington had struck the sand bar full on and was bogged.

Captain Lindsey arrived at Providence at sunset. He moored the *Hannah* and looked up his friend, John Brown, a prosperous merchant and shipowner in the town.

"John," Lindsey said, "the *Gaspee*'s sprawled on Namquit Point like a pig across a plank—and there she'll be till flood tide."

"Ah?" said Brown. "And that's after midnight, eh?"

"It's three o'clock in the morning."

"Well, well!" Brown looked thoughtful. "They say she's Hancock's sloop. John Hancock of Boston."

"She might be," said Lindsey. "I couldn't swear to it. But whosever she is, she's stranded now."

"Thank you for telling me." Brown smiled. "You know, Lindsey, I'm getting a very amusing idea."

"I thought you would," said Lindsey.

John Brown went to his dock, where he spoke to Mr. Whipple, his shipmaster. "I've a little errand to do tonight," he said. "Something's come up quite suddenly. I want eight of my longboats readied by ten o'clock, Mr. Whipple. Eight pairs of oars to the boat, and the oars muffled."

Mr. Whipple said, "Aye, sir. You'll have 'em."

At dusk, a man in a clownish sort of costume walked down the Providence Main Street, rattling a drum and chanting a monotonous singsong.

"The *Gaspee*, the *Gaspee*," he chanted. "Stranded on Namquit Point she lies and won't get off till flood tide floats her. For more about poor *Gaspee*, go you to James Sabine. The *Gaspee*, the *Gaspee*—"

James Sabine was another Providence merchant who, like John Brown, had been plagued by the meddlesome Lieutenant Duddington. Within the hour Sabine's house was visited by many curious people, and at ten o'clock sixty-four men stepped into Brown's eight boats and glided away in the darkness. A few of them were armed with guns, the rest had slingshots and quantities of small round paving stones in their pockets.

The longboats reached Namquit Point at one-thirty in the morning.

"Who goes there?" cried the watchman on the *Gaspee's* deck.

The Providence men were silent and rowed closer.

Then Duddington loomed beside the watchman. He was in his nightshirt and he flourished a pistol.

"Be off!" he shouted. "Hold off!"

The longboats came on, Duddington fired and was greeted with a shower of stones and the flash of a musket. He groaned and fell. The watchman shouted and three of the crew ran from below deck and carried their commander to his cabin.

There were no further shots, either from guns or slings. The *Gaspee* sailors huddled in their quarters. The Providence men boarded the ship and took possession—quietly, even politely. One of them, a young medical student, went to Duddington's cabin and bandaged his wound.

"A bullet in the thigh," he said. "A clean wound, you'll be all right."

"What are you going to do with me?" Duddington asked, writhing with pain and impotent anger.

"Take you to Pawtuxet," said the medical student, "and leave you there. You can get a doctor at Pawtuxet."

"And my crew?"

"They can go ashore," the student said. "If they go now, they can wade. If they dally about, the tide will be in and they'll have to swim for it."

At two-thirty everybody was off the *Gaspee*. Then her captors set the ship afire. The sky reddened with the flames' reflection, and people for miles around could see the glow and smell the smoke. When the last embers sputtered out at the water's edge, the longboats glided back to Providence.

The next day, Governor Wanton issued a proclamation: the burning of the *Gaspee* was a crime; the persons responsible for it would be arrested, tried and punished. A reward of five hundred dollars was offered "for the perpetrators of this villainy, the money to be paid upon the conviction of any one or more of them." Let those citizens who had knowledge of the matter come forward and confess it!

Governor Wanton waited. He was positive that at least a thousand people must have such knowledge; some of them would covet that reward. A secret shared by so many could not be kept.

The governor waited for weeks, months. No one came forward to confess. He probed and queried. The citizens of Providence said they didn't know and couldn't imagine who had burned the *Gaspee*. It was a mystery, they said.

After six months had passed, Governor Wanton wanted to abandon an investigation in which he could make no progress at all; but British statesmen said that the King, Parliament, the flag of England and the royal navy had been insulted and must be conciliated. In January, 1773, a commission of inquiry was sent to Rhode Island; and two rewards, both larger than the first, were posted: five thousand dollars for the apprehension of the leader in the "villainy," twenty-five hundred for clues resulting in the arrest of the leader or any of his accomplices.

"When taken, the culprits will be extradited for trial in England," said the commissioners.

Then Stephen Hopkins, the venerable chief justice of Rhode Island had something to say. Hopkins was a patriot, and courageous.

"Extradited? Never!" Hopkins asserted. "Extradition is

illegal. If any person should be charged with burning the *Gaspee*, he will be tried here, within the colony's limits."

But the offers of reward, the threats of the commissioners were to no purpose, and the splendid firmness of Stephen Hopkins was unnecessary. Not a solitary arrest was ever made, not a clue divulged. Providence folk kept the secret, their lips sealed.

In June, the commissioners admitted that they were baffled, and the investigation was dropped.

The *Gaspee* incident had its effect upon all those Americans who had thought, wishfully, that England's attitude toward them was softening. The mulish obstinacy of the Crown seemed out of all proportion to the facts of the crime—if it was a crime. A ship flying the King's colors had been destroyed—a ship that the colonists generally believed to be the confiscated property of an American. And how many times had Lieutenant Duddington pursued and overhauled law-abiding traders like Captain Lindsey of the *Hannah?* Hadn't Duddington merely been given a dose of his own medicine—a strong dose, though not too strong?

The *Gaspee* incident, said the colonists, had been just a squabble between a bumptious young British naval officer and a few Rhode Islanders whom he had bedeviled often and unmercifully. Why make a mountain out of a molehill?

"It's over and done with now, anyway," they said. "A thing of the past, it should be forgotten."

In London, the King fumed. The colonists might find excuses for the rashness of a handful of Rhode Islanders; George III could not, nor did he seek them. He blamed all the Americans for the misdoings of that handful. They were all incorrigible. They must be brought to heel!

10

●●●●●●

"Boston Harbor a Teapot!"

In 1773, King George had in his cabinet two men who would help him to humble the uppish Americans. They were Lord North, England's prime minister, and the Earl of Dartmouth, the foreign minister. Both had the habit of deferring to their monarch in everything.

But how was the humbling to be done? Well, there was the tea tax—and it was a very good time to be thinking of the tea tax, for the British East India Company was just about to go bankrupt.

The British East India Company was an old and hallowed corporation; its charter had been granted by Queen Elizabeth in 1600. For almost two centuries it had carried on an enormously profitable trade with the Far East and had held a monopoly on this trade. One of its chief commodities was tea exported from China and sold in the British Isles and the English colonies. Tea exported by rival corporations in Holland and elsewhere might be smuggled into America—indeed, it was, quite frequently. But only English tea could be legally sold to British subjects.

The decline of tea-drinking in the colonies had at first puzzled and then dismayed the East India Company. For seven years, chests of tea for which there was no American market had been piling up and rotting in London warehouses. The company owed the British government great sums of money.

Now the King and his pliant ministers devised a marvelous plan by which this trouble could be remedied—and other troubles with it. The plan was laid before Parliament and passed as the Tea Act of 1773.

By this Act, Parliament reduced the price of tea from twenty shillings a pound to ten, and allowed the East India Company to export it directly from the Orient to the colonies, without having to stop at English ports en route. In America, the tea was to be received by agents whom the King appointed. The agents were not to pay any duty, and they would have a monopoly on the sales. The duty of threepence a pound would be paid by the colonists as a tax and—here was the Act's wonderful feature—the tax would be collected by the customs officials when the ships were unloaded, before the tea was sold! Thus, the colonists would be taxed, whether or not they were tea-drinkers!

In this way, so Parliament said, many interests would be well served. The colonists who did drink tea would get it (and the very best tea, bohea!) at an absurdly low cost. The London warehouses would be cleared of tons of old stock. English merchants would no longer have to compete with American merchants; smuggling shippers would be ruined. And the King would prove his power to tax, his sovereignty.

A clever arrangement all around! The British East India Company immediately started vessels laden with a half-million pounds of tea for New York, Philadelphia, Boston and Charleston, South Carolina.

The colonists were irked. A clever arrangement? It was a snare, a ruse. They saw through it and vowed to have none of it. Why should they be exploited to stave off the bankruptcy of an ages-old corporation that for generations had enriched the English Crown?

Liberal-thinking Americans said that the agents selected by the King were all prominent Tories, men who had fought every proposal that might have given the colonists some voice in their government. Colonial merchants were against monopolies of any variety. If the tea market could be swallowed up, so could the market for cloth, wine, shoes—anything. Business in America would be dead as a doornail! Retail shopkeepers wailed that they were being robbed of their livelihood, that they might as well pull down their blinds, lock their doors and set out for the almshouse!

In Boston, Samuel Adams nodded sagely. The King, said Adams, was harking back to the Declaratory Act passed by Parliament in 1766 and never repealed. Americans had foolishly overlooked the Declaratory Act; it gave Parliament power to make laws binding the colonists "in all cases whatsoever." The Stamp Act, the Townshend Acts had been repealed. The Declaratory Act remained on the statutes, and now the King had resurrected it.

"And we have no recourse through our legislatures," Adams said. "As Thomas Hutchinson told us: rebellion is, and always has been, the only alternative to submission."

The tea ships were due in American ports in the autumn of 1773. If they landed and unloaded, the colonists would be liable for the tax. They must not land! In New York and Philadelphia, the protest was so great that the King's agents there resigned. The patriots of Charleston were thinking of how they could prevent a landing—and in Boston, the mobs were out once more.

Three ships—the *Dartmouth*, the *Eleanor* and the *Beaver*—were coming to Boston. Weeks before they were sighted, the Sons of Liberty were considering ways of dealing with them. On November 5, five hundred "free men" of the town con-

gregated under the Liberty Tree, heard Samuel Adams de-
nounce the Tea Act and then paraded to the store of Richard
Clarke, one of the Tory agents, bidding him resign his
agency. When Clarke refused, his house was wrecked. Two
of Thomas Hutchinson's sons had also been granted agen-
cies; the same demand was made on them. The Hutchinson
brothers, like Clarke, were unyielding and suffered the same
damages.

The Governor himself was at his country home in Milton.
He said the tea ships would land. Oh yes! Parliament's ruling, the King's wish, would be complied with to the letter.

Thereafter, public meetings were almost a daily event in
Boston. Not only the rabble, but doctors, lawyers, merchants,
women and schoolchildren went to Faneuil Hall to listen as
Samuel Adams or John Hancock or Joseph Warren ex-
pounded the evils of taxation without representation. There
were also smaller, very exclusive meetings at night at the
Green Dragon Tavern, the Salutation Tavern, or in the house
of Benjamin Edes, the Tory-baiting editor of the *Boston
Gazette*. These night meetings were for the younger members of the political caucuses. Lendall Pitts, the son of a Boston importer, was their chairman.

The young men seemed to enjoy their gatherings. They
came away laughing and murmuring that Lendall Pitts was
an ingenious fellow, with something funny up his sleeve!

The *Dartmouth,* containing one hundred and fourteen
chests of tea, arrived in Boston harbor November 8. Her
owner, Francis Rotch, was told by a delegation of patriots
that if he unloaded, it would be at his peril. Rotch was a
Bostonian. Months earlier, not foreseeing what he might let
himself in for, he had leased the *Dartmouth* to the East India
Company. Now he ordered his captain to moor at Griffin's
Wharf, but he was worried about his cargo: unless delivered

to the agents within twenty days, the tea would be confiscated by the customs officials.

And what then? thought Rotch. Shall *I* have to pay for it?

The next morning, Bostonians awoke to a town which overnight had been plastered with posters, inviting them to a meeting at Faneuil Hall at ten o'clock. "Every friend of his country, to himself and posterity is now called upon . . . to make a united and successful resistance to this last, worst and most destructive measure of administration!" the posters screamed.

By ten o'clock more than a thousand people were crowded into Faneuil Hall. Samuel Adams was on the rostrum.

"We must send back the *Dartmouth* as a challenge to the royal prerogative!" he said. "Let us vote to send it back!"

But the crowd was so big and so excited that a vote could not be taken. Adams adjourned the meeting, telling the people to reassemble in the afternoon in Old South Church, where they would have more room.

At the afternoon meeting, twenty-five hundred citizens voted to send the *Dartmouth* back to England, with her cargo intact and not a penny of tax paid on it. Only one man disagreed—Dr. Thomas Young, a youthful friend of Lendall Pitts's.

"I'm not for sending the ship back!" cried Dr. Young. "I'm for throwing the tea overboard!"

But even to Sam Adams, this suggestion seemed rather drastic. It was decided that Rotch would have to get the *Dartmouth* out of the harbor, and that guards would be on the water front to see that the tea chests were not opened. Paul Revere and five other couriers for the Sons of Liberty then volunteered to ride to neighboring coastal towns, to make sure that no tea ships were landed elsewhere in Massachusetts.

On December 2, the *Eleanor* entered Boston harbor; the

Beaver came a few days later. Each one had a hundred and fourteen chests of tea in their holds. Both moored at Griffin's Wharf beside the *Dartmouth.*

Governor Hutchinson was now a very perplexed man. Here, with a fleet of British battleships anchored nearby, and British troops garrisoned on Castle Island—here were three lawfully commissioned vessels, fetching not smuggled goods but perfectly legitimate merchandise valued at £18,000 in English money, that could not land at this port!

The captains of the three lawfully commissioned—and marooned—vessels were beseeching Hutchinson: "What must we *do?*"

He repeated the statement he had made so often: "The tea cannot be returned to England until the duty is collected. I have given orders to harbor officials that no tea ship can sail outward from Boston unless its captain has papers to show that the tea tax has been paid."

On the afternoon of December 16, seven thousand people were in Old South Church, crowding the benches, standing in the aisles, packed solidly in the galleries. The weather was raw and dreary, a thin rain falling. The church windows were gray, steamy with moisture.

From his seat behind the pulpit, Samuel Adams peered— and gloated. Never before had the citizens of Boston been so determined in their opposition to a royal edict. Surely they were well started now on the path toward rebellion. And they must go all the way! Adams thought. There must be no faltering.

Today they were waiting for Francis Rotch, who had driven out to Milton for one last talk with Governor Hutchinson. If Hutchinson would permit the *Dartmouth* to sail out of the harbor and back to England, cargo and all, this incredible riddle could be solved. It was seven miles to Milton, a long, wet trip for Francis Rotch, a long wait for the people in the church.

As they waited they had been entertained with speeches by Adams, John Hancock and Josiah Quincy. Bostonians liked speeches, but as the church darkened and candles were lighted, they yawned, stretched and dozed.

At six o'clock, Rotch appeared, looking disconsolate, his boots and trousers muddy. He said, "Mr. Adams, I didn't get it. Governor Hutchinson won't give me the clearance papers. The governor stands by the King. The *Dartmouth* stays where she is till the tax is paid."

The church was hushed. Samuel Adams stepped to the pulpit. "This meeting can do nothing more to save the country," he said, and his tone was cool.

But instantly a voice whooped from the gallery: *"To Griffin's Wharf! Boston harbor a teapot tonight!"*

John Hancock got to his feet and shouted: *"Let every man do what's right in his own eyes!"*

Then everybody was up, making for the doors: *"To Griffin's Wharf! Boston harbor a teapot!"*

Less than an hour later, a hundred and fifty men were running pell-mell down Griffin's Wharf. They were disguised as Mohawk Indians, their faces smeared with lampblack or burnt cork. They carried axes, tomahawks and knives. The rain had stopped. The three tea ships swung gently on the water.

Lendall Pitts was the leader of the men; he divided them into three groups. With one group, Pitts went aboard the *Dartmouth.*

"Light up!" he said to the mate. "Hand me your keys!"

The mate handed over his keys, and a cabin boy got lanterns.

"To work, Mohawks!" Pitts cried. "We haven't much time!"

The tea chests were hoisted from the hold to the deck,

broken open and the tea spilled into the harbor. On the *Eleanor* and the *Beaver*, axes rang on metal, wood crackled as it split. Toiling, the men grunted and sweated. Tons of tea slid over the rails, floated like seaweed, staining the water brown. On the wharf were thousands of people, all silent.

By nine o'clock the work was finished. The Mohawks sprang from the ships' decks, formed into ranks and, trailed by the watchers, tramped up the wharf toward the State House. Somebody produced a fife and played it—shrill and roistering music.

As it happened, Admiral John Montague, commander of all the British battleships stationed in Boston harbor, was spending that night at the home of a Tory friend of his, whose windows looked on Griffin's Wharf. Montague had seen the whole thing, and he had not said one word to his friend, to anybody. But when the Mohawks were under his window, he popped out his head.

"Well, boys," he called, "you've had a fine evening for your Indian caper. But, remember, you've got to pay the piper yet!"

Lendall Pitts laughed, and answered. "Come down, sir, and we'll settle the bill in two seconds!"

Admiral Montague shut the window with a loud bang.

11

●●●●●●

A New Governor

Samuel Adams and John Hancock felt that the Boston Tea Party had been a great success; but more tea ships were on the way to American ports. Early in 1774, they sent Paul Revere to New York to tell the Sons of Liberty there what could be done with unwanted cargoes.

Revere was thirty-nine years old, sturdy, stouthearted—a versatile man, a useful man in any venture. His hands, small but strong, were as capable at grasping the bridle of a galloping horse as at the delicate molding of gold and silver ornaments. His father, Appolos Rivoire, emigrating to Boston from France in 1716, had changed the family name and established the business which Paul had inherited.

In his dark good looks and florid complexion, black hair, flashing black eyes under thick arched brows, and in his quick, animated gestures, Paul Revere's French ancestry was shown; but his mother was an Englishwoman. He was Boston-born; America was his country.

"Bold Revere," so he was known at the Salutation, the Green Dragon, wherever the colonists' cause was championed. "Bold Revere," and the adjective was meant as a tribute to him.

As a consequence of the message from Boston, New York patriots were on the alert and when the English brig *Nancy* arrived at the East River dock, they garbed themselves as Indians and drowned her freight of tea before it could be unloaded. By comparison with the first one, this Tea Party was a minor offense, but it further incensed the King, who already had launched a program of grim revenge.

The King, his ministers and Parliament now believed that Boston was at the bottom of every new outbreak against the Crown. Speakers in the House of Commons described the town as "a nest of locusts," whose brash inhabitants "should be knocked about the ears." In the House of Lords, Bostonians were said to be "knaves," a "blight," the scum of the earth. London newspapers called Boston "a cankerworm in the heart of America," "a rotten limb that must be lopped off." The East India Company said Bostonians were thieves; they should be made to reimburse the company for its losses.

And the sentiment of the English people was altering, too. Before the Boston Tea Party, there had been many Englishmen who were friendly toward the colonists, a larger number who thought the King's methods might be a bit harsh, and still more who were indifferent to the whole matter of colonial rights. Now these groups were consolidated, all siding with the King. The Americans were behaving abominably, even treasonably—down with them!

Benjamin Franklin was in England at this time—and uncomfortably aware of the shifting viewpoint. Franklin had been working for a reconciliation between the colonies and the Crown. Never imbued with the passion for independence that drove men like Samuel Adams, Franklin visualized a great empire in which England and America should be equals and at peace.

This ideal was very real to him. He had talked with Lord North and the Earl of Dartmouth about it.

"A government," he said, "of two Parliaments, one here in London, a second, but not subservient, lawmaking body in Philadelphia."

He thought the ministers were interested—they seemed to be. Then, just as his hopes were rising, news of the Boston Tea Party was received in England. He was astounded. He felt, and said, that such violence was dreadful, a grievous error on the part of his countrymen. The East India Company should, of course, be compensated, and he added that the colonists were truly not insurrectionists. No, no! They abhorred the thought of war!

But the statesmen to whom he said it made no comment, shrugged or turned away. Soon he was informed that the King had dismissed him from his place as postmaster general for America.

So, in the spring of 1774, Dr. Franklin was suddenly out of a job, out of favor, shunned and lonely among people with whom he had long been congenial. But still he stayed on in London, fearing war, praying that he might help to avert it.

In March, Parliament passed a bill closing the port of Boston to all ships except those bringing military stores to the continent. The Port Bill would become effective June 1, and would be stringently enforced until the East India Company was paid £18,000 sterling for the spoilage of three hundred and forty-two chests of tea. The purpose of the bill was obvious: to starve the citizens of Boston into obedience. George III signed it with dour pleasure, as if he heard his mother's murmuring voice: "Be a king, George! *Be a king!*"

The situation of Bostonians was now grave, indeed. How must they face and withstand it? The geography of the town would put them at a disadvantage from the very start. Boston was pear-shaped, built on a peninsula and connected with the main coast of Massachusetts only by a narrow neck of land, or isthmus, that at high tide was almost submerged. With water all around, British battleships in the harbor and redcoat troops on Castle Island, the town would have little or no contact with the outside world; its people would be quite literally in danger of starving. They must prepare as though for a siege, perhaps a long one.

Paul Revere saddled his big gray horse again and rode out to ask for help from the other colonies.

The Port Bill was the first item in the King's program to reduce Boston; more items were to follow. Rapidly Parliament passed a series of measures known in England as the Coercive Acts, in America as the "Intolerable Acts." The seat of the Massachusetts legislature was moved from Boston to Salem. Henceforth, all members of the legislature would be appointed by the King, all judges and court officials by the royal governor. No public meetings of any kind could be held without the written consent of the governor, obtained in advance of the meeting date. At such meetings no question could be discussed except those of which the governor approved.

Then Parliament passed the Quebec Act, a measure that was not one of the Coercive Acts, but was nonetheless intolerable to the colonists. Among its several provisions, the Quebec Act extended the border of Canada southward to the Ohio River, thus granting to Canada huge tracts of forest and prairie that Virginia, Connecticut and Massachusetts had thought belonged to them by virtue of their charters.

Americans in every section responded warmly to Boston's appeal. Their sympathies were touched—and their instinct for self-preservation. The punishment inflicted upon one town could be inflicted on all. When and where would Parliament strike next? Who would be the next to feel the King's vindictive wrath?

During those spring weeks of 1774, gifts poured in upon Boston: barrels of dried fish, casks of olive oil from neighboring towns, wheat, rye and corn, donations of money from Connecticut. Charleston, South Carolina, sent hundreds of bushels of rice that could be stored as food or sold for cash. New York sent a large flock of sheep and a written guarantee: "We will supply you with enough food to last out a siege of ten years."

Bostonians were consoled by the generosity of their friends. It was encouraging to know that the colonial Committees of Correspondence were tightening their system of communication, that patriots in Rhode Island and New York were tentatively planning a Continental Congress to be held as soon as possible—that at Williamsburg, George Washington had told the Virginia House of Burgessess: "If need be, I will raise one thousand men, subsist them at my own expense and march myself at their head to the relief of Boston."

Yes, all this upsurge of fellow feeling was gratifying. But meanwhile, the town was confronted by still another misfortune. The King had decided to impose military law in Massachusetts.

Thomas Hutchinson, the King thought, had not been a proper royal governor. Hutchinson was faithful, but, in the King's opinion, not a good executive, too often outwitted by a blustering rabble. For instance, the withdrawal of British troops had been a gross mistake—how weak of Hutchinson to accede to it! The King felt that perhaps no American, even the most loyal, was fitted to govern in the provinces. An Englishman was required, a soldier, with plenty of soldiers behind him.

Having made his decision, the King asked for Hutchinson's resignation and appointed General Thomas Gage to close the

port, and thereafter to keep Boston in the correct state of
humility and subjugation. The two regiments on Castle Island would be returned and re-installed, and more troops
would join them.

"A sufficient garrison," said the King. "Sufficient for anything."

Military law? To Bostonians, it seemed a final disaster.

The British transport *Lively* brought General Gage, his
staff of officers and a brigade of infantrymen, grenadiers and
marines into the harbor. They disembarked at high noon of
May 17, a day of pelting rain and chill winds slashing from
the northeast.

The King had said that Gage must be welcomed with
pomp and ceremony. Accordingly, Thomas Hutchinson had
ordered a banquet at the State House and had gathered a
reception committee, consisting of himself, the Crown officials in Boston and a sizable array of Tory gentlemen. Also
the militia companies had been called out to parade on the
Long Wharf. By eleven o'clock, the streets were filled with
people, most of them wet and shivering, a few sheltering
under umbrellas—those newfangled contraptions of oiled silk
or linen spread on clumsy ribs of whalebone.

With his committee, Hutchinson waited at the end of the
wharf. This was his last hour of authority. Soon he would
sail for England to give the King an accounting of his years
—his stormy years!—as governor. He would not be sorry to
go, but he hoped the King would forgive him his faults of
administration, whatever they were, and allow him to come
back. America was his native land. Boston had always been
his home.

Standing in the drenching rain that sluiced off his shoulders and ran down his collar, Thomas Hutchinson contem-
plated the possibility of being exiled from home forever.

It is hard, he thought. Very hard!

But now General Gage and his retinue were descending the gangplank, resplendent in scarlet coats, chalk-white breeches, glittering gold braid. The guns on all the British ships roared a salute, bugles sounded.

Hutchinson and Gage bowed, shook hands, formally, courteously. Drums pounded, and the two governors, the new and the old, walked together up the wharf and up King Street, to their elegant banquet in the State House.

William Dawes was in King Street that morning. All the bustle and to-do, the crowd, the soldiers, reminded Dawes of the day six years ago when, with his friend Paul Revere, he had watched a similar pageant. He looked for Revere now, but didn't see him. No, Revere would be out somewhere, as he usually was, riding hell-for-leather. Dawes himself sometimes rode for the Sons of Liberty. It was great fun, he thought, carrying messages.

He heard his name spoken—"Well, Billy?"—and turned to see another of his friends, Dr. Joseph Warren, tall, fair-haired, handsome—said to be the handsomest man in Boston.

"Well, Doctor?" Dawes said, "It's happening again, eh? Just like in '68. Only Gage didn't stay then. Now he's to be with us for good."

"Or for ill," amended Joseph Warren, faintly smiling.

"Things don't get any better, do they?"

"On the contrary, Billy, they get worse."

"Yes," Dawes said. "Martial law, and they'll ram it down our throats—or try to. A thousand lobsters came on the *Lively*, two thousand will be moved back from Castle Island—"

"And more will be sent from England," said Warren. "God knows how many more."

"For us to feed and quarter. For the colonial militia to welcome! What a mockery, eh?" Dawes grunted, his lip curled disdainfully. "The militia made to kowtow to these Britishers —and scarce a one of them that's not of our kind and won't rally to us at the drop of a hat. And the people, they're all for us."

"No," Warren said. "Not all, Billy. Not even most. The division here is about the same as everywhere in the colonies. If the hat were dropped, we'd have one-third of the people with us. One-third would be against us, and the rest neutral."

"Tories, king-lovers! Clods!" Dawes scowled, then brightened. "But the hat'll be dropped, Doctor."

Warren nodded. "I think so. I see nothing else for it, though I couldn't guess in what circumstances, or how soon."

12

●●●●●●

A Continental Congress

General Thomas Gage had come to Boston to close the port
—and close it he did, exactly as the King had specified, at
midday, June 1, with a thunder of artillery. The cannonading,
a token of royal power, served as a mourning signal for hundreds of thousands of Americans. Virginians observed the
day by fasting; throughout all the colonies, windows were
curtained, bells tolled dolorously, sermons were preached
and prayers said in the churches.

The people of Boston had known that with the sealing of
the port, they would be in sore straits, but the reality was
more severe than anything they had imagined. The commerce of the harbor, the wharves and the water front had
been the blood stream that sustained and nourished them.
Now the shipyards suspended operation, the warehouses
were shuttered, the docks deserted. Stevedores, carpenters
and sailors were thrown out of work. Shops, large and small,
had no customers, their clerks no employment. All trade was
paralyzed.

And yet no voices were heard suggesting that the King,
Parliament and the East India Company be appeased. In ad-
versity, Boston was bleak, but not apologetic, not begging for
pity or pardon.

The King had decreed that Salem was to be the new capital of Massachusetts and the official residence of the governor. Therefore, General Gage went to Salem, leaving the command of the British troops in Boston to Colonel Hugh Percy.

Percy was a young man, an English earl, the son and heir of the Duke of Northumberland.

"Be resolute with the citizens," Gage told Earl Percy, "but don't harass them unduly. They feel put upon, and why grind them into the dust? I see no sense in that."

Gage himself was middle-aged, cautious, of a normally placid temperament. A captain on his staff had once said: "The general is a sociable fellow." The comment had amused him.

"Sociable? Perhaps I am," he said.

In one capacity or another, Gage had spent a good many years on the North American continent. He had campaigned with Braddock during the French and Indian War, participating with Colonel George Washington in the arduous retreat from Fort Duquesne. After the war, he had been governor general of Canada, until 1763, when he became commander of all the British troops in the English colonies.

He knew that some of his contemporaries, and probably the King, were scornful of the colonials as soldiers, but he had fought side by side with the militiamen and believed them to be rough, tough and brave into the bargain. He didn't think quite so well of their officers; it seemed to him that Washington had been their only military man worthy of the name. Washington had undoubtedly shown great ability. But now the militia companies seemed to be poorly trained, and, of course, not equipped at all.

As for American civilians, Gage had always had a kindly feeling for them; he had married an American girl, Margaret Kemble, of an aristocratic New Jersey family. He felt that he understood these people. He hoped to pacify rather than antagonize them. Some were wily and intractable; he would set spies to uncover them, then chastise them as individuals. He did not believe that the good should be made to suffer with the bad.

He had written to the King: "If the government is *firm*, the Americans will prove very meek." This was the theory to which he would adhere.

Gage had read Thomas Jefferson's *Summary View of the Rights of British America*. He spoke of it to Earl Percy.

"It is an essay enumerating what the people see as the King's acts of oppression, and asking that a minister of American affairs be included in His Majesty's cabinet. Jefferson is a liberal. But even Jefferson recognizes that the colonists *are* British subjects. I think they'll all ultimately accept the fact of their dependence upon England. Even the Bostonians will knuckle under. Why, what else *can* they do, Colonel?"

Earl Percy made a wry face. "Begin a shooting war?"

"Oh, surely not," Gage said. "It would be suicide."

"I'm told that the militia companies are almost wholly disaffected," Percy said. "And more and more of these 'minutemen' are being recruited. They are auxiliary bands, but in league with the militia. They all sing this patriotism tune. In case of war, they would combine, unify."

"War?" said Gage. "No, the Americans may be willful, but they're not crazy. They'll not begin a shooting war." He paused, and said, "Nor will we."

The legislators of Massachusetts resented the moving of their capital from Boston to Salem. On June 17, they met in Salem to register a protest.

Gage was surprised to hear that they were meeting. It was the privilege of the governor to summon the legislators. He had not summoned them—hadn't been notified of the session until it was in progress. He sent his secretary to dissolve it. The secretary returned shortly, looking piqued.

"The door was locked against me, sir," he said to the general. "Mr. Samuel Adams is presiding. He had locked the door. I stood on the stairs and shouted your order as loudly as I could, but got no response—save from a jabbering parcel of townsfolk who had collected on the pavement. They laughed at me."

Gage bit his lip and frowned. The word "meek" darted into his mind. Was he mistaken about the people? Oh well, let them have their session. What was the harm in it? He must be patient, and later he might dissolve the legislature entirely, permanently—if he had to.

Behind their locked door, the legislators framed their protest, and also a letter that would go to all the colonies, recommending that the First Continental Congress be convened at Philadelphia in September. Then they elected five men as the Massachusetts delegates to the Congress: Samuel Adams, John Adams, Thomas Cushing, James Bowdoin and Robert Treat Paine.

Someone asked whether the governor might not interfere, forbidding the journey of the delegates.

Samuel Adams replied for the five, saying simply, "We shall make the journey."

The summer months of 1774 were hot and dry, and not easy for General Gage. He attempted to organize a governor's council, but of the thirty-six men he appointed, only sixteen would serve, and these were so taunted and tormented by their neighbors that they had to go to Boston where the garrison could protect them. It was the same with other officials whom Gage would have appointed. He found it impossible to hold court in the colony. Judges, sheriffs, justices of the peace, either flatly refused the positions he offered, or assumed them and then would not perform their duties.

In July he abandoned the idea of trying to conduct the government of Massachusetts from Salem, and went back to Boston. British troops were steadily accumulating there, an army of more than five thousand. The old barracks in the town would not accommodate this inflow.

"We must have new barracks built," Gage said to Earl Percy.

"If we can get the carpenters and masons, sir—"

"I'll hire civilians. Hundreds of them were deprived of their jobs by the Port Bill. Poor devils, they'll be glad to have some coins jingling in their pockets again."

But the carpenters and masons of Boston preferred idleness—and poverty—to the work and decent wages General Gage promised them.

"*Meek!*" he said to himself. "Well, I'll have laborers brought from New York—or Halifax. Yes, I'll send to Halifax for Canadian artisans."

He sent to Halifax, and the Canadians came. Then mysterious accidents happened to his building materials. Barges transporting bricks for the barracks sank without any visible cause. Wagons loaded with lumber were upset or bogged in country lanes. Straw for the soldiers' beds caught fire and burned to nothing.

"It will be November before we get our own men roofed over," he said to Percy. "And even so, we'll have to put many of them into private homes."

"Isn't that legal, sir?" Percy asked. "Sanctioned by the Quartering Act?"

"Legal, yes. The Quartering Act stipulates that the town must feed and house our troops. But the people will hate it!"

As a dashing and gallant young officer, Earl Percy was popular with the Boston Tories, and was often entertained in their homes. He said now, "I think the Tory citizens might not object to having British guests for a while."

"Perhaps not," said Gage. "But my orders from London are that the Tories must not be so inconvenienced."

In August, disturbing rumors cropped up like clouds of gnats. Gage's spies told him that the colonists were buying (or more probably stealing) ammunition and muskets which they hoarded in outlying villages.

"They're said to have a stock of gunpowder in the colony magazine at Charlestown, just across the river from us," Earl Percy reported. "The stuff won't be there much longer; the Sons of Liberty are taking it off, a little at a time, to caches farther from Boston. And in Cambridge, they have two cannon, fieldpieces, obtained by hook or crook. It would not be difficult to retrieve them, sir."

"I suppose the colonists would argue that the things are not stolen, but purchased with money from the province treasury," Gage said. "Thus, they're the property of the people."

"And the people will use them against us," said Percy.

Gage pondered. Retrieve the gunpowder, the cannon? It could be done, but would that be wise? No, he thought not. He was anxious not to play the tyrant. He would wait for more information.

The Crown authorities did not forbid the journey of the Massachusetts delegates to the Continental Congress in Philadelphia. As Samuel Adams had predicted, the five men left Boston on the morning of August 10. Their departure in hot summer sunshine from the home of Thomas Cushing had a gala air about it. John Hancock had lent them his coach for the trip, a huge and magnificent vehicle, polished to mirror-like luster, the wheels striped in yellow and red, drawn by four sleek horses, escorted by outriders.

The delegates were in good spirits and their best bib-and-tucker. To everyone's astonishment (even his own, it seemed) Samuel Adams appeared in the Cushings' parlor wearing a brand-new suit of claret-colored broadcloth and a ruffled shirt. His hair was neatly trimmed and tied in a beribboned queue. His shoes had silver buckles, and he carried a gold-headed cane.

"Why, Cousin Samuel, you are a veritable peacock!" exclaimed John Adams at sight of him.

"A gift from the Boston Sons of Liberty," said Samuel. "See, the emblem of the organization engraved on my coat buttons and the head of my cane."

"And I must say the finery well becomes you! You should have your portrait painted just so."

"I shall," said Samuel. "My friend Hancock has arranged for it. I am to sit for Copley, the same artist who painted Hancock himself."

"The famous Copley? It is in claret-colored grandeur that posterity will remember you," said John, smiling.

Samuel's answering smile was sardonic. "If posterity remembers me at all. And that is a thing that does not bother me, John," he said. "Nor you, either, I fancy."

The wives and families of the delegates, many friends and members of the Sons of Liberty were at Thomas Cushing's house to wish the travelers godspeed. The ladies had provided a light luncheon of biscuits, fruit and punch. John Hancock and Josiah Quincy made speeches, and toasts were drunk to the delegates' health and the success of their mission.

Then farewells were said, the coach door slammed, the driver cracked his whip—and away they went, rattling through the Boston streets, cheered by patriot citizens, scoffed at by Tory pedestrians, and on orders from General Gage, ignored by the patrolling British regulars.

For almost a month, they would go onward, by road, ferry boat and barge, to Connecticut, to New York, to New Jersey, and come at length, rather disheveled but hopeful, to the big city of Philadelphia.

The Congress convened September 5 in Carpenter's Hall. Georgia was not represented, but the other twelve colonies had sent their ablest men. John Adams, looking around him at the opening session, thought that never before had there been such a mobilization in America. He named to himself some of its leaders: Stephen Hopkins of Rhode Island, Roger Sherman of Connecticut, John Jay of New York, John Dickinson of Pennsylvania, John Rutledge of South Carolina. And what a remarkable delegation Virginia had contributed! Patrick Henry, Peyton Randolph, Richard Henry Lee and, most sagacious of them all perhaps, George Washington.

"I believe Washington is the best man we have," said John Adams to Samuel. "He is substantial, mentally and physically vigorous, a tower of strength."

"Yes, yes," Samuel said. "Everybody is here, I see—everybody but Ben Franklin and Thomas Jefferson."

"Franklin is still in England," said John.

"And as for Jefferson, the Virginia burgesses thought him a bit too radical, I daresay." Samuel grimaced and smiled. "I shall miss Jefferson. I feel that we'll need him."

Meeting daily, the Congress produced an Address to the King, an Address to the People of England, and a Declaration of Rights that stated, once again, the grievances of the colonies and recited thirteen acts of Parliament to which Americans could not submit.

The language of these documents was respectful. No demand for independence was made. There was no intimation that the colonies might resort to arms to regain the rights which the King had taken from them. The Congress asked only for relief from unfair taxation and a share in governmental responsibility. Then, to give the petitions some degree of force, it was voted that an association of the colonies be formed, and that the old compact to import no goods from England be renewed.

But would the King heed the petitions?

Certainly not! thought Samuel Adams. "What we have done is merely to repeat ourselves like parrots," he told his Massachusetts colleagues. "How many times have we said and written these very things? And what have they accomplished? Has the King ever heeded our puny weeping and wailing? No, nor will he now!"

"We have shown the King that we can unite," said Thomas Cushing.

"It is not enough," Samuel Adams said. "A union passive, without power, is nothing. We shall see that George III pays no attention to our declaration, our mealymouthed addresses. Of course not! None at all!"

The Congress adjourned on October 1, just as disheartening messages from Boston were reaching Philadelphia. A detachment of British soldiers had raided the magazine at Charlestown and carried off two hundred and fifty barrels of gunpowder, all that remained of the Sons of Liberty's stock there. And a second redcoat party had invaded Cambridge and confiscated the town's two small cannon.

So, the final deliberations of the Congress were exceedingly grave. The Massachusetts delegates went home feeling daunted and very gloomy.

13

●●●●●●

Trouble in the Wind

General Gage had reluctantly ordered the raids at Charlestown and Cambridge—but only when the reports from his
spies grew too ominous to be disregarded. Then he sent out
small parties of troops to the two towns. The moving of the
military gear had been quietly done, there was no resistance,
but the effects of it were amazing.

Somehow and at once, wildly distorted tales of strife and
bloodshed flashed from village to village, and by noon of
the next day four thousand Massachusetts men were trudg-
ing toward Cambridge, believing that the British were laying
siege to the countryside.

Hastily, Gage sent out more soldiers to disperse the patriots.

"Reassure them!" he instructed his officers. "Tell them my
purpose is to preserve the peace, not to break it!"

For several days, while the Americans were being con-
ciliated and turning back, rather sullenly, to their homes,
Gage was much worried, and then he wrote a letter to
London.

"The situation here is inflammatory, and my position rela-
tively weak," he wrote. "I shall fortify Boston and the isthmus

known as the Neck, but in the event of war, I could not successfully ward off an attack. If New England is to be reduced as the King desires, I must have ten thousand additional regulars."

But still he did not really expect an attack, and when the excitement had subsided, he said so to Earl Percy.

"There will not be war, Colonel, unless we precipitate it. These people know that their resources are at most crude and limited. They know that England is the greatest nation in the world."

Earl Percy was silent. To him, the colonists seemed a set of rascals, sly, hypocritical, conniving. They should all be disarmed, Percy thought—and the sooner, the better!

During the summer, Gage had permanently dissolved the Massachusetts legislature; but the legislators met anyway at Salem in October, again behind barred doors, and constituted themselves as a Provincial Congress. Gage promptly issued a proclamation stating that the acts of the Provincial Congress were treasonable and prohibiting the people from complying with them; but the Congress continued to meet, through the autumn and winter. A Committee of Safety was created, headed by John Hancock, and measures were adopted for the calling out of the militia and minutemen in times of danger.

In fact, the patriot people of Massachusetts were now endeavoring by every available means to improve those resources which Gage had said were crude and limited. The militia was reorganized and new officers named. An appropriation of money, £15,627 sterling, was voted and raised, with which to buy guns, bayonets, mortars, bombshells, spades and pickaxes, messbowls, canvas for tents. Non-perishable food, such as flour, dried peas, beans and rice, was bought and carefully stored. In candlelit kitchens, family groups—men, women and children—cast bullets and made cartridges.

Sometimes the means were stealthy. There were many instances of theft and smuggling. Farmers, driving home from marketing their vegetables in the town, concealed stolen muskets and ammunition in their wagon beds and were gleeful at evading the British guards on Boston Neck. Gunrunning became a sort of game for the colonists. One night, the King's battery at Charlestown was stripped of its guns; on another dark night, four cannon vanished from Boston Common and were later hidden in haystacks many miles distant.

Gage did what he could to cope with these conditions. He saw the militia drilling, awkwardly but doggedly, on village greens, and often he paraded his own companies—"for exercise," he said, but with the thought that the villagers would be overawed by the superior discipline of the redcoat veterans. He put some of his officers to patrolling and mapping the roads around Boston. Others, disguised in civilian clothes, frequented inns and taverns where Americans might be drinking and gossiping. He got Tories to spy for him, and bribed them for their services.

In February, 1775, he sent Colonel Leslie of his staff with two hundred and forty infantrymen to Salem, to seize a few brass fieldpieces in the arsenal there. "If I don't get them, the villagers will!" he said to himself. But Salem was warned of Leslie's approach, and the British found a matching force of townsfolk and minutemen waiting for them. After a little maneuvering and exchange of challenges and insults, the Britishers faced about, foiled and frustrated, and marched back to Boston.

The "inflammatory situation" in Massachusetts was worsening day by day; and Gage was irritated to learn that it was almost as bad everywhere. The Virginians seemed to be virtually begging for war. Gage would have liked to throttle that eloquent gadfly, Patrick Henry!

On March 23, in the House of Burgesses, Patrick Henry delivered the most incendiary speech of his career, a short speech but so gripping, with a climax so dramatic, that his hearers shouted, cheered and wept.

". . . We must fight!" stormed Patrick Henry. "I repeat it, sir, we must fight! An appeal to arms and to the God of Hosts is all that is left us. . . . Gentlemen may cry, peace, peace—but there is no peace. The war is actually begun! The next gale that sweeps from the north will bring to our ears the clash of resounding arms! Our brethren are already in the field! Why stand we here idle? What is it that gentlemen wish? What would they have? Is life so dear, or peace so sweet, as to be purchased at the price of chains and slavery? Forbid it, Almighty God! I know not what course others may take; but as for me, give me liberty, or give me death!"

Liberty—or death.

Yes, that was the feeling of Americans in 1775; and Thomas Gage, a gentleman who in his heart wished for peace, peace, was ever more perplexed to know what course *he* must take, considering both his natural impulses and the allegiance he owed his King.

As he fretted and vacillated, pulled this way and that, he received a communication from Lord Dartmouth. Parliament had declared the colonies to be in a state of rebellion. The King had said publicly: "I am not sorry that the line of conduct seems now chalked out. Blows must decide whether the American colonists are subject to England or independent."

Sighing, frowning, Gage scanned the official document. So

the King was not opposed to the idea of armed conflict? Not
at all! George III was impatient to see the rebels start it.

Spring came on unusually early and beautiful that year of
1775. Massachusetts people said they couldn't remember a
lovelier season. The sun shone, the rain was soft. By mid-
April the frost was out of the ground, farmers were sowing
and planting, the breeze wafted a fragrance of fresh-plowed
soil and blossoming orchards.

Paul Revere had ample chance to enjoy the good weather
as he went about on his errands for the Sons of Liberty, the
Provincial Congress, the Committee of Safety. He was very
busy. Indeed, all winter he had been in the saddle most of
the time, riding through snow and sleet. He had neglected
his shop. Oh well! There were things more important now
than the silversmith's trade.

In addition to his chores as courier, Revere had for months
directed a small private ring of spies—his "mechanics," he
called them. These stout fellows were friends of his, artisans
like himself, but out of work, utilizing their leisure in keeping an eye on the doings of the British soldiers in Boston.
Circulating, drifting, haunting the water front, sauntering
around the British barracks, the fortifications that Gage
was building on the Neck, the "mechanics" picked up many
morsels of interesting news. They reported their discoveries
daily to Revere or to Dr. Joseph Warren, who then forwarded
the information to the organization or persons it most concerned.

On Saturday, April 15, the "mechanics" on the Long Wharf
noticed that boats belonging to the British transport vessels
in the harbor were being repaired, recaulked and tied up
under the sterns of the battleships. This was odd. Were the
boats going somewhere?

When Paul Revere was told about the boats, he suspected

that an expedition was in prospect. To East Cambridge by water and thence by land to Concord? Yes, he thought, so I'll wager!

It had been said in patriot circles that General Gage was planning to arrest John Hancock, Samuel Adams and Dr. Warren and bring proceedings against them as traitors. For several weeks, the three men had been in Concord, attending the Provincial Congress which had just adjourned. Hearing that Gage might have such designs, Hancock and Adams had thought it wise to remain out of reach for a while: they were now in Lexington, secluded in the parsonage of Mr. Jonas Clark, the Lexington clergyman, whose wife was a cousin of John Hancock's.

But Dr. Warren had come home. Dr. Warren said that if Gage wanted to arrest him, he could have done so on March 5, when Warren was the principal speaker at a meeting in Old South Church to commemorate the anniversary of the Boston Massacre. Warren's remarks from the pulpit on that occasion had been emphatic, defiant. They must surely have enraged every Britisher within sound of his voice.

"Gage could have bagged me, Hancock and Adams, all in one throw," said Warren, "for we were all present, and Gage's soldiers were infiltrating the audience. No, I can't believe that the general plans our arrest."

Nevertheless, both the doctor and Paul Revere felt that Hancock and Sam Adams should know about those boats. So, on Sunday, April 16, Revere made a quick trip to Lexington, slipping past the sentries on the Neck (and a neat caper it was) briefly visiting at Mr. Clark's house, and returning to Boston that same evening.

Revere told Dr. Warren that Hancock and Adams took the news calmly, though they agreed that everything suggested some impending crisis.

"Mr. Hancock is traveling in his customary style," Revere

said. "I saw his big coach in the parsonage yard; it's piled with luggage, boxes of papers, trunks of clothing."

"His secretary is with him?" Warren asked.

"Yes, and also his aunt, Mrs. Thomas Hancock, and Miss Dorothy Quincy, the young lady he's engaged to marry."

Warren smiled. John Hancock's romances were eagerly followed by Boston society folk, for he was the most eligible of Boston bachelors. His doting Aunt Lydia wished him to marry and raise a family, and for a ten-year period he had been engaged to Miss Sally Jackson, who then had cruelly jilted him for a rival suitor. Now, for three years, he had courted Josiah Quincy's pretty sister Dorothy. But Miss Dolly, as she was known to her intimates, was whimsical and maybe a bit fickle. She would never fix a date for the wedding. It was whispered that, like so many Boston belles, she had been dazzled by the charms of the titled English officer, Hugh Percy, and that Hancock and Aunt Lydia, horrified by this development, were afraid to let the flirtatious maiden out of their sight.

The next day, Monday, was quiet in Boston. Revere's agents had nothing to report. Tuesday morning was uneventful, too. But in the afternoon, British officers in pairs or threesomes were seen mounting horses and trotting from the barracks areas toward the Neck. The officers wore dark blue cloaks over their uniforms. They seemed casual, laughing and chatting with the guards.

"We're off for exercise," they said. "A whiff of spring, a picnic."

A picnic? The "mechanics" were skeptical, and so was Paul Revere.

Revere could not rid his mind of suspicion, could not dispel the feeling that mischief was afoot. With every hour the feeling intensified. As night closed in, he did not go to his house in North Square to eat supper with his family, but stayed on in his shop, sat at his bench, alone and brooding. Spread on the bench beneath a brace of flickering candles were his tools.

"I should be working," he said to himself, for he had plenty to do. In his desk were a dozen unfilled commissions for jeweled shoe buckles, silver pitchers, ewers, wine buckets and vases. Instead, he was listening, leaning forward, an elbow on the bench, his chin propped on a doubled fist, his ruddy face strained and anxious in the candles' yellow glow—listening for some sound, some signal, he knew would come.

At about seven o'clock Tuesday evening, General Gage in his headquarters at Province House was talking with Earl Percy.

"It is a secret excursion to Concord," he said, "to fetch the military stores."

"A valuable lot," said Percy. "In recent months, Concord and Worcester have been the colonists' main depositories."

"It is a raid," Gage said. "Not more than that."

Percy made no comment. He understood what was meant. The general was as unwilling as ever to precipitate actual fighting. Poor chap! thought Percy, he doesn't want it on his conscience. He's too cautious, always has been. He's between the devil and the deep blue sea: the King and Dartmouth on one side, his instinctive caution on the other.

"Secret," Gage repeated, "and discreet. I'm sending an infantry regiment and the grenadiers. They leave at moonrise and will not be told their destination. They'll ferry across the bay to East Cambridge. Those men who went out this afternoon will see that no patriot messengers or spies are on the road from Cambridge to Concord. If any should be encountered, they will of course be taken prisoner. Lieutenant Colonel Francis Smith will command the troops. As you know, Smith is my senior field officer here."

Again Percy held his tongue. Francis Smith in his prime had been an excellent soldier, but now he was old, fat, slow, sometimes tardy.

"Pitcairn of the marines will be second in command."

"A fine choice, sir," said Percy. "You haven't a better officer than Major Pitcairn."

"If Smith should run into trouble, you will lead out a brigade of reinforcements, Colonel Percy. But I don't think there will be trouble."

"Very good, sir." Percy waited a moment, expecting that Gage might say something further, perhaps a word about the arrest of Hancock and Adams at Lexington. When the word was not forthcoming, he saluted, clicked his heels and made his exit.

As he walked from Province House to his own quarters in the town, Percy saw a little knot of loiterers on Boston Common, where loiterers, at this hour, were not supposed to be. He went nearer, peering at the men through the dusk. They were muttering, chuckling.

"Yes, boys!" said one of them. "Yes, the lobsters have marched—but they'll miss their aim."

"What aim?" asked Percy.

"Why, the cannon at Concord. And who are you, stranger?"

"No matter," said Percy, turning away.

He swiftly retraced his steps, burst in upon Gage and told him what he had overheard.

"Unfortunate!" Gage exclaimed. "Most unfortunate—but we shall just have to go on with it now. If no rebel couriers get out of the town, Smith's march can still be kept a secret."

14

●●●●●●

Perilous Ride

It was ten o'clock when Paul Revere heard the knocking.

Tap-tap-tap.

He rose from his bench, strode to the shop door and opened it. A man stood on the pavement, a dark figure among darker shadows. Revere stepped out, so that he too was shadowed.

"Yes?" he said.

"Dr. Warren wants you, Revere."

"Where is Warren?"

"At home," the man said. "You're to make haste—"

"All right, thanks."

"Something's up. Something big. The regulars are mustering. North Square's crawling with marines, guards in a cordon round the town. Look out for them."

"I'll manage. You hie on."

"Well, then—"

As the man turned and was engulfed in darkness, Revere locked the shop door and started for Warren's house. He was in his shirt sleeves, shivering a little. The night was clear and starry, but cool, a wind blowing from the bay. Later there would be a silver-white moon.

He walked fast. The streets he traversed were deserted, the bordering buildings shuttered and silent, yet he was aware of a quaking sensation beneath his feet, a vibration, like a pulsing in the earth.

At Dr. Warren's, a servant admitted him. Warren was in his parlor, pacing the floor, the lamplight gilding his handsome blond head, his blue eyes glittering feverishly.

"Gage is sending troops to Concord," he said. "A thousand or more. They're forming on the Common now."

Revere nodded. That explained the vibration; it was the tramp of marching men. "They'll board the boats at the bottom of the Common?"

"Yes, and land at Cambridge," Warren said. "It was to be a secret, but somebody gossiped. I had the message an hour ago. We must let Adams and Hancock know, alert the villages."

"I'll go," Revere said.

"Dawes has gone already, Billy Dawes. He was here when the message came. He left immediately. Billy said he'd ride over the Neck to the Lexington pike—"

"Billy's going by way of Roxbury and Cambridge?"

"If he got out of town at all. I'm not sure he did. He said he'd bribe a British sentry, but Gage has packed the Neck with soldiers—"

Revere interrupted again. "He's taking the long route."

"The only route."

"Looping to the southwest, then north? No!"

"But how else—"

"I'll row across the Charles from a cove near Barton's Point, get a horse on the east bank, and beat Dawes to Lexington."

"Impossible!" Warren said. "Impossible!"

"No, it isn't," Revere said. "Sunday evening, coming back from Mr. Clark's, I stopped at Charlestown. I saw Conant,

the militia colonel there. I told Conant I might soon be need-
ing a horse on his side of the river. He said he'd have one
for me. I'm to signal with lanterns in Christ Church belfry;
it's high, the highest belfry in Boston and the top windows
look east to Charlestown—"

Now Warren interrupted, almost angrily: "Row? In what?"

"A skiff. I've got one, bought it last December. Joshua
Bentley and Tom Richardson have been hiding it in Bentley's boatyard. I shouldn't wonder but they'll want to row
me across."

"The King's frigate *Somerset* is anchored near Barton's
Point, Revere."

"Yes, I'll have to dodge the *Somerset*."

Warren paced restlessly. "Lanterns! Will Conant see them?
It was Sunday you talked with him; this is Tuesday."

"He said he'd watch every night. He promised."

"But hanging the lanterns? Who'll do that?"

"I think I know the man for it—and I'd better be talking
to him." Revere grasped Dr. Warren's hand and shook it
hard. "No fear, I'll get to Lexington tonight."

"God help you," said Warren fervently.

Hurrying from Warren's house, Revere sought out Robert
Newman, a youthful and enthusiastic member of the Sons
of Liberty, who lived with his parents in the neighborhood
of North Square. Newman was surprised but flattered to be
drawn into Revere's confidence.

"Listen, Bob," Revere said. "John Pulling, a vestrymen of
Christ Church and a good friend of mine, has the key to
the belfry. Find Pulling, he'll let you in."

"And I know where the lanterns are," said Newman
eagerly. "In a cubbyhole below the belfry stairs. I'll tend to
it, Mr. Revere, and glad to! Don't you worry!"

Then Revere went home to get his boots and a warm coat.
Pausing at the bedroom door, he looked in at his sleeping

children. He loved his children—his "lambs," he called them.

His wife Rachel, clad in a quilted wrapper, was at his shoulder. She said, "This isn't like your other trips, Paul."

He smiled. "Not quite, I guess."

"No, it's the real thing, it's war!"

"Maybe not, Rachel."

"It is! The beginning of war. You've said it would come, and it has." Trembling, she clung to him. "I'm frightened. If they catch you, they'll kill you!"

"They'll not catch me."

"Oh, Paul, be careful! Do be careful!"

He kissed her, and said, "I will."

Wearing his heavy riding boots and a woolen surtout, he slipped out of the house. His dog, a brown spaniel, leaped at him and licked his hand.

"Down!" he said. "Down!"

Whining reproachfully, the dog slumped to its haunches.

Revere walked to the alley and emerged on a rear street. He felt something brush against his legs—the dog!

"Back, you wretch!" he said. "I'm not going hunting. Back!"

The dog stopped, then went back through the alley, tail drooping.

Revere strode on at a rapid gait, making several turnings. The tension of the town was increasing, he thought. Lamps glimmered in many houses. British soldiers patrolled in squads. From North Square echoed a metallic clatter of sabers, muted shouts.

He hurried across a vacant lot and came to the street where Richardson lived. Richardson and Bentley were cronies; yesterday he had told them to be at Richardson's house tonight —and there they were!

"Your boat's launched, all tidy," Bentley said. "We'll man

the oars, Tom and I. You brought the cloth for muffling them, I reckon?"

"Cloth!" Revere ejaculated. "I forgot it!" He was dismayed —and in the same instant he knew that he had also forgotten his spurs! He cursed himself for a fool, a dolt.

"Now, now, it's not that bad," said Richardson. "I've got no spurs, nor has Josh. But cloth? Hey, hold on a minute."

Revere grumbled. He couldn't afford a minute. Time was precious. "Hold on? Why?"

Richardson winked, darted into his house and reappeared, a bundle under his arm. "My sister's petticoat," he said. "Lucky I've got a sister, eh—and with a petticoat to spare."

Running in and out of alleys, avoiding the corners where the British might be patrolling, they reached Bentley's boat-yard on the reed-grown river bank. They tore the flannel petticoat into strips and swathed the blades of two pairs of oars. They stepped into the skiff—and heard footfalls padding softly behind them.

"Hist!" Bentley said.

The reeds parted, and Revere's dog slid, snuffling, down the steep bank to the water's edge. Tied to the dog's collar were the forgotten spurs. Laughing, Revere leaned from the skiff, patted the dog's nose, untied the spurs and clipped them to his boot heels.

"Rachel must have found them after I left," he said. "She'd know I wanted them; she sent them to me. Well, shove off, Josh!"

The *Somerset*, a frigate of sixty-four guns, rocked gently at midstream of the Charles. Her sole reason for being in that vicinity was to keep Bostonians, especially men like Bold Revere, immured in Boston.

Bentley and Richardson gave the battleship a wide berth, detouring around it, dipping their oars with strong, even strokes, easing their little craft toward the east shoreline. When the skiff nudged shore, Revere jumped out, murmuring his thanks. The rowers waved and shoved off again.

Revere climbed to level ground. Colonel Conant was waiting for him. With Conant were several militiamen and Richard Devens, a member of the Committee of Safety.

"You saw the lanterns?" Revere asked.

"Oh, yes," Conant said. "Very nicely done. A couple of flashes; more would have been too many. And here's your horse—a loan from John Larkin."

John Larkin was Charlestown's richest citizen. His horse was a fine one, young and slender, rather small, but muscular, satin-skinned and groomed to perfection. Revere inspected the horse approvingly, adjusted the stirrups to proper length, tested the snugness of the girths, the set of the bit.

"British officers were on the Concord road this afternoon," Conant said. "They were in and about Cambridge for hours."

"I saw ten of them at Menotomy," Richard Devens said. "Our committee met there today. As I drove out of Menotomy at sundown, they stopped me. They were armed and mounted, in long cloaks—a thin disguise! They asked me the location of Clark's tavern in Lexington. I concluded they had their orders mixed up; they meant Mr. Clark's parsonage, where Hancock and Adams are staying. So I said I didn't know any such tavern, and I sent a Menotomy man toward Lexington. But I'm afraid my man didn't get through. They probably trapped him."

Revere swung into the saddle. "What time is it now?"

"Just eleven," Conant said. "Look sharp for those chaps, Paul."

"I will," Revere answered. "I'll manage."

He touched spurs to the horse's flanks, and was on his way.

Charlestown, like Boston, was on a promontory, attached to the mainland by an isthmus known as Charlestown Common. Beyond were two roads, both leading to Lexington. Revere was familiar with them both; one was very sandy and rutted, narrower than the other, but shorter, and he took it, riding through a desolate stretch of salt marsh and clay pits, the Charles River on his left, the Mystic River on his right.

He admonished himself that he had ten miles or more to go and must not push too hard, lest the horse should tire. A steady canter, that was the ticket!

The moon had risen, starkly illumining the marsh. Soon he glimpsed the tree where an iron cage dangled. The cage contained a heap of bleached human bones, the shattered skeleton of a slave named Mark, who twenty years earlier had been hanged there in chains by the master he had tried to escape. The wind swayed Mark's cage; the bones rattled.

Was it, Revere wondered, a reminder to all slaves of the penalty for defying authority? He averted his eyes and scanned the unfolding road ahead, swiftly covered several miles—and saw his progress blocked.

Two horsemen lurked under the branches of a tree. British officers! The moonlight revealed their cockaded hats, the holsters at their belts. He knew at once that they had seen him, and that the road was too narrow for passing.

Now one of them started toward him. He jerked the rein, spun about, pressed his spurs. His horse responded with a burst of speed. Doubling back, he galloped for the alternate road. A glance over his shoulder assured him that he was outdistancing his pursuer. A second glance, and he saw the Britisher's horse blundering into a clay pit.

Revere laughed aloud. For all their smartness, these fellows hadn't learned the hazards of the Massachusetts terrain!

Following the curve of the Mystic River, he galloped into Medford village, halted briefly and wakened the captain of the militia.

"The regulars are out, bound for Concord!"

The militia captain sprang to attention; he would summon his men.

From Medford to Menotomy the road was sparsely fringed with houses. Revere knocked at almost every one.

"The British are marching! Get the warning round!" he cried, and was rewarded by the abrupt flare of lamps in windows.

So much, he thought, for Thomas Gage's prized secret!

At midnight he dashed into Lexington. He had ridden nearly thirteen miles. His horse had not faltered, but seemed as mettlesome as ever. What a splendid animal, what joy to have such a mount!

Mr. Jonas Clark's parsonage was about a quarter-mile northeast of the Lexington green; Revere made for it, still galloping. Approaching the rambling, gabled dwelling, he was astonished to see guards, eight of them, in the front yard. They were minutemen and their sergeant was William Munroe.

"Munroe!" he cried. "The British—"

"Yes, I know," Munroe said. "They've got spies out. Solomon Brown was in Boston today. He met up with a bunch of them at Menotomy. That's why we're here. We thought the parsonage should be watched—"

Revere had not the time or patience to hear more. "I've got to tell Adams and Hancock—"

"They're in bed. Mr. Hancock hustled Sol Brown on to Concord, but we've not seen hide nor hair of Gage's boys. Got sidetracked, I guess, skipped Lexington. The folks are all asleep. Mr. Clark said not to disturb them. No noise in the yard, he said—"

"Noise!" Revere roared. "*Noise!* You'll have noise enough before long! The regulars are marching!"

John Hancock was not asleep; he came to the front door. "Revere? Come in."

Revere went into the house. "Billy Dawes hasn't reached you?"

"Dawes? No," Hancock said. "What—"

Breathlessly, Revere told his story. The British were marching, not a scant handful of roving officers bent on spying, but regiments of soldiers, a thousand or more. This was no unsubstantial rumor; it was true, true!

His entrance had roused other occupants of the parsonage: Samuel Adams, Mr. Clark and his wife, Hancock's Aunt Lydia and Miss Dolly Quincy. They all clustered about him, in excitement, consternation—and a variety of robes and dressing gowns over their nightclothes.

Hancock was pale, but determined to join the Lexington men who would now be gathering on the green. "Where's my sword?" he demanded. "Fetch my gun, somebody!"

"Oh, no!" wailed Aunt Lydia. "You mustn't *fight*, John."

"No, no!" said Miss Quincy.

"Yes, ma'am! Hush, Dolly! The scoundrels must be stopped. My place is on the firing line!"

Adams spoke, characteristically wry and calculating. "And that would please Gage very well, John. It's exactly what he'd like best. You, on the firing line, a target for his first volley. We must get away from here, you and I. To Woburn—"

"Sneak off to Woburn? Never." Hancock bellowed. "I'm not a coward!"

"Nor am I," said Adams. "But I'll not play right into Gage's hand."

Hancock's reply was another bellow: "My gun! My sword!"

In the midst of this argument, William Dawes arrived at the parsonage door. He said he had ridden sixteen miles, without accident or sight of Gage's spies; the patriots were mustering in all the towns and villages.

"I'm going on to Concord," said Revere.

"Good!" Dawes nodded. "I'll go with you."

Mrs. Clark looked at the two couriers. How weary they must be, and how hungry! "Mr. Revere, Mr. Dawes, you must have something to eat."

"Well, maybe—" said Revere.

Dawes grinned and said. "Well, thankee ma'am. Just a bite."

15

●●●●●●

"Stand Fast!"

Revere and Dawes left the parsonage at one o'clock in the morning. Food had refreshed them. Their horses had been rested. Trotting briskly through Lexington, they glimpsed lights, heard voices and knew that the people were all up and stirring.

At the outskirts of the village, the clop-clop of hoofs sounded behind them, and they were overtaken by Samuel Prescott, a young doctor of Concord. Dr. Prescott was active in the Sons of Liberty organization. Tonight he had been calling on his sweetheart, Miss Millikan, who lived in Lexington.

"I'm going home," he said. "Let me ride with you, Revere."

"We may be nabbed, Sam," said Revere.

Prescott smiled. "I'll risk it."

So, quickening their pace, they went forward, three abreast, until they were halfway to Concord. Then Dawes and Prescott dropped back to alert the inhabitants of a farmhouse. Revere forged ahead—and saw two British soldiers plunge from a clump of bushes, bearing down on him.

"Stop, damn you!" the soldiers shouted. "An inch farther and you're a dead man!"

Revere's thoughts raced. Two Britishers, with pistols—but three Americans could surely handle them! He yelled for Dawes and Prescott: "Come up, boys! Spies!"

Dawes and Prescott came at the gallop—and more Britishers loomed from the bushes. Four, six!

Revere yelled again, at the top of his lungs: "No! Keep clear!"

Dawes swerved sharply, his horse rearing. Then he went pounding back toward Lexington. Prescott, too close to turn, found himself in the circle of hostile figures and brandished guns that surrounded Revere.

A British major commanded the party. "Get off the road, Yankees!" he said. "Into that pasture with you. Get going or I'll blow you to bits!"

The pasture at the roadside had gates which had been opened. Revere and Prescott walked their horses through the gates. Revere could think of nothing else to do, for he was not armed. Prescott had a whip, which he lifted menacingly—and received the painful gouge of a pistol barrel in his ribs.

Low walls of stone bordered the pasture laterally. At the far end was a little grove of trees. Suddenly Prescott cried, *"Put on, Revere!"* and rushed to the wall, jumping his horse over it, making his escape. At the same instant, Revere applied his spurs, rushed for the grove and saw, too late, redcoats among the trees.

The soldiers snatched his bridle, dragged him from the saddle, kicked, poked and prodded him. One in a sergeant's uniform grasped him by the collar.

"What's your name, Yankee?"

"What's yours?" Revere growled.

The sergeant shook him. "Spunky, ain't you? Be nice and we'll not hurt you. We're not looking for rebels. We're here to trap some of our deserters."

A lie! Revere thought. Bluff and bluster! Well, anybody can bluff. "I know why you're here," he said, "but the regulars aren't on this road. They never got to Cambridge, their boats grounded in the swamp. Oh, you'll soon see troops, I grant you. Companies, regiments, and *all colonials.*"

Four other prisoners were penned in the grove: Solomon Brown, the messenger John Hancock had dispatched from the parsonage; two Lexington men who disclaimed any knowledge of either British or American troops; and an obviously harmless and terrified peddler of pots and pans. After a while, the British major herded them all on to the road.

"Release these four, sergeant, they're of no consequence," the major said, pointing. "This one is Paul Revere, a Boston silversmith, a courier for the traitors, and slippery as an eel. Watch him and if he tries to bolt, kill him."

The sergeant saluted. "Yes, sir."

It seemed to Revere that the major was uncertain about how to proceed, but presently he set out slowly in the direction of Lexington, his party trailing. Revere was allowed to ride, but the sergeant held the bridle, leading him. When they were within a half-mile of Lexington, a shot rang out.

The major halted. "What's that for, Revere?"

"To rouse our people," Revere answered.

"Who's shooting? Where?"

"It could be anywhere," Revere said.

The major seemed more uncertain, then said, "Get down, give the sergeant your horse."

Revere got down. The sergeant took his horse, and away they all jogged, toward Lexington, leaving Revere alone on the road, staring after them.

So he was free! But bewildered. He might as well go back to the parsonage, though it would be a long walk and very tedious in his heavy boots. He wondered how Prescott had fared, and Billy Dawes, and where they were by this time. He thought of how he had boasted (not once, but twice) that he could "manage."

Oh yes, he had "managed," good and proper; managed himself into a ridiculous mess and lost a fine horse to a British lobster!

That horse! Always and forever, Paul Revere would remember that magnificent horse, and sing its praises.

The occupants of the parsonage were all fully dressed when he got back there, and Hancock's secretary, John Lowell, had come over from his room at Buckman's Tavern. The Clark children were up, looking dazed and frightened. Mrs. Clark's father had sent a cart from his farm, which was nearby, to rescue the children and Mrs. Clark too, and the other ladies. Mrs. Clark, wringing her hands, said she didn't know whether to go with the children or stay and help her husband, who was hiding the family valuables in the garret and cellar.

Revere was in the yard with Mr. Lowell, when Mrs. Clark drove off with the children to Grandfather's farm.

"I've had a phaeton harnessed," Mr. Lowell told Revere. "I think Mr. Adams will win the argument. Mr. Hancock will go with him to Woburn or some place of safety. However, the alarm may have been false. Captain John Parker had his men on the green by two o'clock, and there they've waited. It's well past three now. Parker's beginning to think of dismissing them. Perhaps the British aren't marching at all."

"Yes, they are," said Revere. "They're coming."

At four o'clock, it was known that Captain Parker had ordered a dismissal. Some of the men had gone home, more of them had followed Parker to the tavern, where they continued to wait. Parker had scouts out; soon there might be definite news.

At last Adams prevailed on Hancock to leave the parsonage.

"Fortunately, the phaeton is ready," said Mr. Lowell.

"What about old Mrs. Hancock and Miss Quincy?" Revere asked.

Mr. Lowell sighed. The ladies had refused to budge. Miss Quincy wouldn't go, nor Mrs. Hancock without her. But Mr. Clark was also staying. Mr. Clark said the danger was not great, he could adequately protect them.

At four-twenty, Hancock, Adams and Lowell climbed into the phaeton.

"Come, Paul," said Hancock. "There'll be chores for you at Woburn."

Pleased at the idea of having something to do, Revere squeezed in beside Mr. Lowell. They had driven only a short way on the road to Woburn, when Mr. Lowell exclaimed: "Mr. Hancock, that trunk of papers, your records of the Provincial Congress! It's in my room at Buckman's. I must fetch it. I'll borrow the parsonage chaise and come after you."

"But the trunk weighs a ton," said Hancock. "You'll never move it by yourself, Lowell."

"I'll help with it," Revere offered.

"Very well," said Hancock. "And fetch my aunt and Miss Quincy in the chaise, Lowell. Tell them they must come, don't take no for an answer. And something else—the salmon that's in Mrs. Clark's cupboard. An exceptionally fine large fish. It was to have been broiled for my breakfast, I shall have it for dinner."

Now it was five o'clock, the sun rising.

Captain John Parker's scouts had reported: the alarm was not false, of course not! The church bell had tolled, muskets had discharged a warning round, young William Diamond had beaten his drum. The militia and minutemen of Lexington were once more on the green.

From Lowell's window, upstairs in the tavern, Paul Revere surveyed the patriots. How few they were, and how gallant! At this height, Revere could see the winding road south of the green. His eye caught the shimmer of scarlet and gold, bobbing black helmets, the glint of the sun on steel bayonets. Like a flowing stream, he thought. Like a long many-hued undulating ribbon—so terribly long!—reaching back into dim distance.

"This is the trunk," said Lowell. "We must hurry."

They carried the trunk downstairs and across the green, passing between the ranked men who were so quiet, rigid, as if carved from granite. Captain Parker was speaking to them. Revere could hear him plainly.

"Stand fast," Parker said. "Stand fast . . . don't molest them, without they begin it first."

At the parsonage, and the trunk disposed of, Revere found another upper window and leaned from the sill. Aunt Lydia came and thrust out her bonneted head.

"Is it really the British, Mr. Revere?"

"Yes, ma'am, the regulars. They've halted just beyond the green. We can't see much, all these trees—"

There was a pause that seemed an eternity. Then Parker's voice: "Disperse, men." Then shouts, a multitude of furiously shouting voices—and an explosion.

A gun had been fired. A British gun? A patriot gun? Revere didn't know, he couldn't see.

And then the blast of many guns.

"An attack!" Revere cried. "They've attacked us!"

Something whizzed by Aunt Lydia's ear. "What's that?"

"A stray bullet, ma'am. It hit the stable—"

Aunt Lydia shrieked and drew in her head.

So it's war, Revere thought. He must get back to Boston,

his family, his duties with the Sons of Liberty. He would be needed at home now. Somehow he must "manage" the journey. Ride, if I can, he thought; and if not, shanks' ponies!

Probably he would find Dawes there before him. He wasn't worried about Billy Dawes. Dawes was ingenious, daring, he wouldn't have been captured. Fling Billy Dawes from a precipice and he would land on his feet—and live to a ripe old age.

But what of Prescott? Had Prescott reached Concord?

In the phaeton, John Hancock and Samuel Adams bowled along toward Woburn. Adams was smiling, his expression rapt, blissful, the look of a dreamer who sees his dream becoming dear reality.

"Oh, what a glorious morning is this, John," he said.

"Eh?" said Hancock. "The weather, you mean? Yes it is, beautiful, lovely."

16

●●●●●●

Morning in Concord

At about the time that the British major was releasing Paul
Revere, a solitary guard patrolled back and forth in front of
the Concord courthouse. Since the previous Sunday, Colonel
James Barrett of the Concord militia had stationed a man
there every night. Colonel Barrett didn't like the look of
things. Trouble was surely brewing. It was his job to see that
the munitions and supplies hoarded in and around the town,
and mostly at his own farm, were not tampered with.

The colonel hadn't particularly wanted this responsibility
—hadn't wanted to assume command of the combined militia
and minutemen, either. He was sixty-five. Too old, he had
said, and not in the best physical condition for military service. But the people of Concord just wouldn't listen to that.
James Barrett was so respected, so wise. He could advise
them, couldn't he? They would spare him the more strenuous activities and do his biddings.

Tonight Amos Melven had the courthouse post. His instructions were to pull the bell rope if he saw or heard anything that seemed unusual. Pacing, occasionally gazing up
at the moon, Melven felt lonely, a little drowsy, chilled. The
day had been mild, but now there was a breeze, crisp and
penetrating.

Melven buttoned his coat, yawned—and gasped. A horseman was galloping into town, galloping past the millpond, into the square, right to the courthouse.

Who—? Melven squinted his eyes. Why, it was Sam Prescott, and he was hollering: "Amos, pull that rope!"

Melven was plumb amazed. Sam Prescott wasn't a courier, never had been. He was a local boy, a smart young doctor. Tuesday nights he rode over to call on his Lexington ladylove. What was he doing here at this hour, hollering like crazy and his horse all of a lather?

But even as he wondered, Melven moved to the bell rope and jerked it.

Clang-clang! Clang-clang!

As the final brassy peal shuddered into silence, Sam shouted: "Tell Barrett the regulars are out, headed for Concord! I'm going on!"

The regulars? "Is it a raid?" Melven asked.

"A raid—at least!" Prescott replied, and then waved his whip and rocketed away.

Well! Melven thought of what he himself ought to do. Run home and warn his folks, maybe? But the bell would have warned them—and everybody. How often Colonel Barrett had drilled it into them: "When that bell rings, grab your gun and make for Wright's Tavern, corner of the square!"

Melven had his gun, so he ran to the tavern.

The first Concord man to answer the bell's alarm was the Reverend William Emerson. Melven wasn't much surprised at this. Many New England clergymen were ardent patriots, none more so than William Emerson. But he must have hurried to get to the rendezvous so quickly! Though Concord wasn't such a big town, it was all spread out, the houses widely separated. Mr. Emerson's house, the manse, was quite a piece up the road, near the North Bridge.

Melven and Mr. Emerson solemnly shook hands and talked

a little, low-toned. Melven said he reckoned the British were
after the stores, and that for the last few days Colonel Barrett and some of the boys had been hiding them in different
places. Melven thought, hopefully, that the Concord men
would number eighty, maybe nigh on to a hundred, ". . . if
they all show up," he said.

"They will," said Mr. Emerson. "And we'll have reinforcements. The whole countryside is rallying."

Very soon Colonel Barrett appeared at Wright's Tavern,
astride one of his plowhorses, and looking not a bit old, but
sturdy and energetic. By three o'clock, the Concord company was mustered, full-strength. Nobody really knew what
was happening, or what to expect. Colonel Barrett sent
Reuben Brown riding toward Lexington for news. Then he
appointed Major John Buttrick to take temporary command,
while he supervised the more thorough concealment of the
cherished stores.

Mr. Emerson had spoken prophetically: the whole countryside was rallying. Messengers were speeding like a relay
team from village to village. Colonel Conant and his Charlestown friends had roused their neighborhood. Somebody had
streaked to Lynn and Woburn, somebody else to Billerica,
Acton, Danvers. Bedford had sent the tidings to Andover,
Dedham, Sudbury. Before noon the people of Worcester
would know.

The earliest reinforcements to arrive were thirty-eight
militiamen and two captains from Lincoln. At about half-
past five, Reuben Brown was back with his report.

There had been fighting in Lexington, a battle! Reuben
had ventured close enough to hear a tempest of shooting and
to learn that men had been killed on Lexington green. Now
the British were marching to Concord.

A battle? Major Buttrick could scarcely believe it. But if

the redcoats were marching to Concord, he would go to meet them!

The road from Lexington, as it approached Concord, curved around the base of a long narrow ridge. This ridge terminated at the square in which were the town's principal buildings: the church, courthouse, three taverns and a few dwellings. From the square, the road angled sharply northeast below a second ridge, then turned due west, crossing the North Bridge over the Concord River.

Buttrick arranged his troops and divided them. The older men and the youngest recruits were to be an "alarm company," he said; Captain Minot would conduct them to the crest of the first ridge, which they were to hold.

"And you, Mr. Emerson, will please to go with Captain Minot," he said.

Mr. Emerson was not pleased. He was being favored because he was a minister. He would have liked to be in the van, in the very thick of things. But a good soldier doesn't question his officer's orders, and it was a compensation of sorts that from the ridge, the patriots could be seen, as they stepped out toward Lexington, their drums and fifes making music.

A small array, but spirited, thought Mr. Emerson. And what grand music!

They advanced a mile and a half. Then the British were in sight, coming on like a vast machine of destruction. Buttrick ordered his men to face about and led them back to the square. He ordered the "alarm company" to evacuate their ridge and to retreat with him to the second ridge, where they would all prepare for resistance.

At eight o'clock the British entered the town. The grenadiers occupied the square and its environs. The infantrymen marched up the slope of the first ridge. A halt was called.

There was a cemetery on this ridge. Walking among the gravestones, Lieutenant Colonel Francis Smith and Major Pitcairn reconnoitered.

Pitcairn had his telescope; Smith had the map of Concord that General Gage had given him—when? Was it only last evening? Smith's nerves were stretched as taut as wire, the effect of that fracas (whatever it had been!) at Lexington. Who would have imagined that veteran troopers could get so completely out of hand so abruptly? Gage would be angry, since his plan had gone askew. He would reprimand Colonel Smith. Next year Francis Smith would be of an age for honorable retirement from the King's army, honorable retirement and pension. He didn't fancy being ousted now, in disgrace, as incompetent!

Smith studied the map. Two bridges were marked on it, both must be secured. South Bridge, he thought, had no strategic importance; one company of infantrymen would suffice there. But Gage had said that beyond North Bridge, by perhaps two miles, was the farm of James Barrett on which a considerable amount of supplies, including cannon, was cached. Six companies must be sent to North Bridge, three to guard it, three to cross and raid Barrett's farm. Meanwhile, Pitcairn's grenadiers could search the town.

Peering through his glass, Major Pitcairn noted that the gathering on the second ridge seemed to be enlarging.

"Quite a lot of people," Pitcairn said. "I believe they're coming from other villages."

"Probably," said Smith. "These Americans never know when to cry quits. It was in General Gage's plan to start Colonel Percy and a brigade from Boston, if support seemed necessary. Several hours ago, I got off a message to Gage, telling him I would welcome help. I supposed Percy would have been here by this time."

Major Pitcairn said that doubtless Colonel Percy would soon appear. He added that the men were hungry and not in the best of humor—though much more tractable than they had been at Lexington.

Colonel Smith was hungry, too—and oh, so weary. He said the men would just have to wait for rations, or forage for them.

Major Buttrick had grouped his Americans as two battalions, and asked Joseph Hosmer to be his adjutant. Hosmer was a cabinet-maker, a quiet man, but popular and influential with his comrades: a Tory had once said that Joe Hosmer was the most dangerous rebel in Concord. He was also modest; he reminded Buttrick that he was only a lieutenant, but at the major's urging, he said he would serve as adjutant for today.

From their elevation, the patriots saw Colonel Smith and Pitcairn in the graveyard. A little later, they saw the grenadiers searching the town, cutting down the liberty pole—that symbol of independence!—stamping in and out of houses, rolling barrels of flour from the mill, splitting open the barrels and spilling the flour into the pond. A quantity of muskets balls was found and dumped into the millpond. The communion silver was taken from the church, and then discarded, dropped carelessly into a vat of soft soap in the street. A fire was kindled in the square. Before it was extinguished, a frame building had burned to ashes.

Major Buttrick and his officers consulted. Joseph Hosmer was for trying to stop such vandalism. William Emerson said, "Let us make a stand! If we die, let us die here!" But Major Buttrick felt that it would be more prudent to retreat to the hill on the far side of North Bridge, for now six companies of British infantry were descending from the cemetery ridge to the road below, and setting off in the direction of the bridge.

At this moment, Colonel Barrett returned to his duty as commander. He said that if raiding was the purpose of the redcoats, as he thought it was, his farm was their objective. With his wife, his children and his fourteen-year-old grandson Jimmy, Colonel Barrett had done everything possible to hide the stores, digging, burying, wheeling the cannon into a ditch and covering them with dirt.

"Yes, we must retreat," Barrett said. "We'll cross the bridge and take up a defensive position there."

So they filed over the bridge, boot heels clicking on the planks, and marshaled on the flat hilltop beyond and above it—all of them except William Emerson, and he went home. His manse was within a stone's throw of the road along which the British would pass; he would protect his family.

At the front door of the manse, Mr. Emerson made his own stand. Retreat? Not another inch!

His wife begged him to come into the house. "William, you will be murdered!"

"No, no, my dear."

He was distraught, anguished at the thought of his church invaded, the communion silver desecrated. And he was curious.

Perhaps it was in William Emerson's thoughts that today, April 19, 1775, was epochal, historic, that its every event should be observed and recorded by some person capable of the task—a person like himself.

The British companies crossed North Bridge; three in charge of Captain Parsons went on to Barrett's farm; three headed by Captain Laurie remained to guard the road.

Captain Laurie had been told that the rebel ranks comprised at most a hundred and fifty men—those ragtag and bobtail louts who had paraded so ridiculously toward Lexington, and seeing the regulars, had faced about and paraded back. But now, glancing up the slope, Laurie was vaguely uneasy. He sent word to Colonel Smith in the town: "The height above North Bridge is fairly thronged. I recommend that more guards be stationed here."

Between nine and ten o'clock the American strength had doubled, then tripled. Two companies of militia and thirty-eight minutemen came from Acton ("And not a one that's afraid!" vowed Isaac Davis, the Acton captain). Threescore militiamen from Bedford brought their flag, a splendid banner flaunting an arm that bore a sword. Recruits came from Carlisle and Chelmsford, from Westford and Littleton.

But they were getting fidgety. Puffs of smoke rose from the square; smoke floated gray and ugly, scarring the blue sky of morning.

"That's my harness shop, I guess," Reuben Brown muttered.

"That's my barn, my stable," said Ephraim Wood.

Joseph Hosmer was indignant. What were they waiting for? "Colonel Barrett, are we to watch the whole town burn down?"

"No," Barrett said, and he drew a deep breath of resolution. "No, boys! We'll march!"

And who would lead the march? Instantly there were volunteers; Barrett chose Isaac Davis of Acton. It was Major Buttrick's privilege to be next in line, but he chivalrously offered the place to John Robinson, the Westford colonel.

"You're my superior officer, Robinson," Buttrick said.

"No, no," said Robinson, equally chivalrous. "I'll be your aide, sir, and go at your side."

They loaded their guns, formed in a column, two abreast.

"Don't fire unless they begin it," Barrett said. "But if they begin it, give 'em all you've got! . . . *Forward!*"

Steadily, soberly, down the hill they strode, keeping step to the tune of *The White Cockade,* shrilled by the Acton

fifers. Reaching level ground, they marched straight toward
the bridge—and saw the redcoats rush back and across, as if
abandoning it.

"Pull up the planks!" cried the British captain. "Rip them
up!"

There was the horrid sound of flailing bayonets and splintering timber.

"Stop that!" Major Buttrick shouted. "Stop it!'

Now the patriots were on the bridge, and running. The
redcoats fired, too fast, wildly, the bullets spattered sizzling
into the river. They fired again, raggedly, then a volley.
Isaac Davis, just lifting his gun to his shoulder, fell dead.
Abner Hosmer, an Acton private, stumbled, sagged and died.

"Fire, boys!" Buttrick ordered frantically. *"For God's sake,
fire!"*

So, as one man, they fired, their bullets smashing in among
the British, killing nine, wounding three, driving the others
in flight from North Bridge and back toward Concord.

17

●●●●●●

The Long Battle

When Colonel Smith heard that Captain Laurie wanted more guards at North Bridge, he ordered out a company of grenadiers and said he would lead it himself.

"I myself will go to Laurie's relief," he said. And so he did. But corpulent and heavy-footed, he had not gone far before he met the panic-stricken, fleeing infantrymen.

Colonel Smith was aghast at this sorry spectacle; he demanded an explanation.

"The Yankees got the bridge, sir," said Laurie.

"Got it? You *let* them get it?" Smith cried.

"There were a great many Yankees, sir," Laurie said. "Too many. The—the engagement lasted only three or four minutes."

"Three or four minutes? Then it was not an engagement; it was a *debacle!* And what about Captain Parsons, the raiders?"

Laurie answered that he had no knowledge of Parsons.

Fuming, chewing his lip, Colonel Smith looked at Laurie's men. Or were they mice? Yes, he thought disdainfully, they were mice, frightened, cringing, utterly demoralized! He pondered what to do with them. Perhaps the best course would be for the grenadiers to trail them to the town square where—surely!—Percy's brigade would soon arrive and the army could be reshuffled and properly arrayed.

"We will return to Concord," Smith said. "Captain Laurie, your conduct has been reprehensible. You will be censured for it."

Shamefaced, Laurie muttered, "Yes, sir."

An hour later, Captain Parsons brought his party back to the village. Parsons said that he had had no difficulty in re-crossing North Bridge; in fact, the rebels had left it. But the search at Barrett's farm had unearthed little of value. Though they had diligently rummaged and ransacked the premises, the raiders had come away almost empty-handed.

"Nothing worth salvaging!" lamented Colonel Smith to Major Pitcairn. "And no word from Percy, eh? Well, we must wait a bit, and meanwhile obtain coaches in which to convey our wounded—to Boston."

At the thought of Boston, the colonel sighed. For months he had loathed the town as a sort of limbo, outlandish, uncomfortable and depraved. Now, strangely, it seemed to him a veritable paradise. He hoped devoutly that he would live to see it again!

Sudden triumph can be as confusing as sudden defeat. After taking the bridge so quickly, the patriots were puzzled and disoriented. What now? Was the fight finished? Probably not, and they were quite willing to go on and finish it. But what was the next objective?

With no plan of campaign, they broke ranks and drifted. Some went to the bridge, picked up the bodies of Isaac Davis and Abner Hosmer, and gently moved them to a shady spot beneath the trees. Others of the men, about two hundred of them, climbed to the hill above the road and, barricading behind a stone wall, reloaded their guns to be ready for whatever might happen. Presently they saw Parsons' raiders passing on the road, the only redcoats to pass within range of vision. The sunshine was warm and bright, the scene placid.

Then occurred an incident that shocked and repelled all who witnessed it. A boy was observed, walking to the bridge where the British dead and wounded were still lying. He was a village boy and alone. He carried a hatchet. He stooped over one of the wounded men, as if to question him. The man lifted his head, as if to reply. The boy swung his hatchet in a crashing blow that split the man's skull. As the man shrieked and swooned in agony, the boy wandered on and was lost to view.

This act of inexcusable brutality would be remembered and frequently cited by Englishmen as proof that the colonists were a savage people, as cruel as ever the Indians had been. Americans would deplore it. The boy, they would say, had no connection with the patriot movement; he was the irresponsible, unpredictable individual to be found in any locality in a time of unusual disturbance.

At twelve o'clock, noon—and no word yet from Earl Percy, no sign—Colonel Smith ordered a retreat of all his troops toward Lexington.

"Without Percy, it may be rather ticklish," he told Major Pitcairn, "but I've no reason for deferring longer."

Major Pitcairn agreed. "Very likely we shall encounter the brigade on the way," he said.

The redcoats formed and marched, and for the first mile were unchallenged. But at the crossroads known as Meriam's Corner, the circumstances changed.

The farm of the Meriam family had become a center on which the Massachusetts militia converged. Men from Billerica, Framingham, Reading, Woburn, Sudbury and Stow had gathered around the farmhouse and spread into the fields, the orchards and woods. And more were coming. In all directions the paths were black with hurrying recruits. And these men were not of a mind to hesitate, withholding their fire until fired upon. Never! They were here to lambaste the British rascals and to keep right at it! At Meriam's Corner, the real battle of the day was started, a battle that would be sixteen miles long and several hundred yards wide.

Colonel Smith saw his danger at once and deployed flanking squads in lines parallel to the road. The Americans promptly opened fire, winnowing and scattering the flankers. The British pushed on beyond the corner, striving to maintain some formation. The Americans, with no concern for rules, ran forward and fired again relentlessly. Over and over this pattern was repeated, mile after torturous mile, the Americans evasive as phantoms, running, pausing, shooting from shelter, from behind houses and barns, walls, rocks and trees. To the British it was a new kind of warfare, one they had never experienced, in which they had not been drilled. They couldn't see their foes, couldn't draw bead on them, scarcely knew from what point they were being attacked.

Why, it was not warfare at all, but something uncanny and mysterious, the work of fiends!

And constantly more Americans were gathering. The galloping couriers had shouted the summons in many towns, large and small, and never vainly. At the alarm, merchants had closed their shops and shouldered muskets, artisans had left their benches, ministers shelved their Bibles, schoolmasters dismissed their classes, wives and mothers had kissed husbands and sons good-by. A thousand men had rallied now, two thousand, three—who could count or name them all?

Somewhere among them was Captain John Parker of Lexington, with his little company reassembled and stanch. Now that infamous dawn assault would be avenged! Captain Parker's gun was hot, his bullets sang as they flew.

Colonel Francis Smith, toiling on, fully aware of his appalling plight, had one satisfaction: he was taking heavy toll of the enemy, not all the blood on the road was British blood, Americans were falling too. But his soldiers were not in columns now. As they neared Lexington, they were a jostling, chaotic mass. Well, something must be done about it! Colonel Smith called a halt.

"What is it, sir?" Major Pitcairn asked, riding up quickly.

"I'm ordering a rear guard to hold back our pursuers while we reorganize," Smith said.

But where were the pursuers? Sitting his horse, Colonel Smith stared, and was perplexed. Not a single rebel was to be seen. They had seemed to rain from the skies; like rain, they had evaporated.

Smoke spurted from behind a rail fence. Colonel Smith clutched his leg. Major Pitcairn's horse plunged, threw him from the saddle, bolted into the meadow and was gone, irretrievably. Major Pitcairn got up and brushed dust from his uniform.

"You're wounded, Colonel! Your leg—"

"Just a scratch," Smith said, wincing but stoic. "A trifle. Major, I am very anxious. We need Percy, Major."

"Yes, sir," Pitcairn said. "And badly."

Errors and misunderstandings had delayed Earl Percy. The officer who was to muster the brigade had been absent from his lodgings when General Gage's order to march at four in the morning was received there, and when the officer got home at midnight, his servant neglected to give him the communication. At five o'clock, Colonel Smith's message to Gage asking that the brigade be sent was mistakenly delivered to someone else. After some time the message reached the general, who then handed it on to Percy, but several hours had lapsed before the brigade could be dispatched.

It was nine o'clock when Percy rode over Boston Neck. He had with him three regiments of infantry, a company of marines, wagons containing food and ammunition and two cannon. His fifers were mocking the colonists by piping *Yankee Doodle:*

"*Yankee Doodle diddle doo*," lilted the fifes,
"*Yankee Doodle dandy!*"

Percy took the route traveled so much earlier by William Dawes, to Roxbury and thence to Cambridge, where he heard that a battle had been fought at Lexington. The stories of the battle were garbled, and Percy did not believe them.

A parcel of provincial bumpkins having the audacity to fight His Majesty's elite veterans? Incredible! thought Percy.

At Menotomy, he heard that the regulars had been "unlucky" at Concord. Well, this was not so bizarre; he could believe it—anyone may be unlucky. Yes, riding north from Menotomy, Percy himself was unlucky. His supply wagons were captured by a band of rebel marauders. He didn't attempt to reclaim the wagons, for the villagers had an insolent air about them, and he did not wish to be diverted from his destination, which was Concord.

So he went on—and very soon was hearing, not stories, but gunfire, and learning to his great astonishment that Colonel Smith was in ignominious retreat!

At about two-thirty that spring afternoon, Percy rode into Lexington. There was now a great sound of guns, louder, recurrent. By straining his eyes, he could glimpse the redcoats approaching from the southeast. As a skilled officer, he knew instantly that his duty would be to cover and expedite their retreat.

Percy stationed his regiments in two lines along the Concord road, thus making an aisle through which Smith's harried column could pass and be shielded. He posted his cannon on a knoll overlooking the green. He saw people skulking around the church, and thought they were mostly young lads and old gray-beards—but he was not sure. He turned his cannon on the skulkers. One blast frightened them off—and considerably damaged the church.

In a few moments, Smith's men were thankfully entering the town through Percy's aisle. Exhausted men, they sank to the ground panting, their tongues lolling out. Colonel Smith was pale, his brow furrowed, his leg bleeding, though he said his injury was slight. Major Pitcairn had got another horse and was, as always, erect and self-possessed.

Earl Percy now took charge of matters, and Colonel Smith was glad to have him do so. Keeping his cannon leveled on the road, Percy allowed the men an hour's rest.

"The rebels are nowhere visible," Percy said. "Perhaps they've relinquished the chase."

"I think not," said Colonel Smith. "I should like to think it—but no, I can't. They will certainly reappear."

At three-thirty, the march toward Boston was resumed, Smith's companies in front, Percy's following and flanking. For a distance of five miles the going was fairly easy. Having rested, the Britishers were in somewhat better spirits. The chances for looting the roadside dwellings were fine, and Earl Percy did not restrain his men. Percy regarded such vandalism with a lordly indifference. Let the redcoats terrorize these countryfolk, if that was their pleasure. Let them steal food, money, trinkets, clothing, furniture, and burn down stables, haystacks and cottages!

Earl Percy's distrust of colonials was deep-rooted and ineradicable. Had not the King said they must be conquered and that no treatment was too drastic for them?

But at Menotomy, the King's men were again in trouble.

Two thousand patriots pressed on Percy there, showering bullets on his flankers. He stopped, wheeled up his cannon and fired—with scant effect. His tormenters eluded him, shifting about with devilish agility, hiding from him, then dodging back to snipe at his heels.

The retreat through Cambridge was a mile and a half of continuous, grueling combat, much of it hand-to-hand. The British soldiers seemed desperately bent on plundering and pillaging, as if this was their sole means of reprisal against their adversaries. They broke into almost every house in the village. They weighted themselves with stolen goods and destroyed what they could not make off with. Maddened by the sight, the Americans changed tactics, rushing from ambush to retaliate fiercely, their clubbed muskets flailing at the bright bayonets. And here, briefly, the British had the advantage, for those bayonets were whetted to an awful sharpness. Americans who sought to defend the houses of civilians were sometimes trapped in them—trapped, gored and their limp bodies trampled upon.

Leaving Cambridge, Percy veered from the highroad and took an angling lane toward Charlestown. Evening was drawing in, the sunset shadows slanted. The lane was shorter than the road, it avoided the bridge over the Charles River. Percy thought it might be safer, by hurrying through it he might shake off the rebels. But they ferreted him out, clung to him like leeches. Twice more he stopped and unlimbered his cannon. The bombardments were futile. Remorselessly he was driven on.

And then it was twilight, dusk, and Colonel Francis Smith's men, in the van of the retreating hosts, were straggling across the isthmus of Charlestown Common to the mainland —into the precincts of Boston.

Boston at last!

For almost twenty-four hours the men had been afoot,

marching thirty-five miles and fighting the greater part of the time and the way, fighting tooth and nail, for their very lives. They were dirty, dog-tired, ravenously hungry, embittered, humiliated—beaten. . . .

"Beaten!" exclaimed General Thomas Gage, glaring at Earl Percy. "*Beaten!*"

"Our casualties were seventy-three killed, one hundred and forty-seven wounded, twenty-six missing, from a total of eighteen hundred," said Percy somberly. "We were sent to confiscate military gear, we have fetched nothing back. The excursion can only be called a failure."

Gage scowled. "But—the colonials? What were their losses?"

"I don't know, sir," Percy answered, shrugging. "How could I?"

"But you judge them to be less than ours?"

"Far less. They will not compare with ours."

"And how many rebels were involved?" Gage queried.

Percy shrugged again, impatiently. "I'm told that in all, strung out from one stage to another, there were three thousand. I can well believe it! They seemed to be everywhere, leaping up from every nook and cranny."

"Messengers had alerted them, I suppose? Couriers?"

"Of course. And the couriers are still riding." Percy paused, and added, "This much I know, sir, and can swear to: the rebels are in earnest and they fight *hard*. They are not to be underestimated. It is a thing we should be foolish indeed to forget."

The colonial casualties were forty-nine dead, forty-one wounded, five missing. The patriots had scored a victory, though as yet they scarcely realized it, or could have imagined the victory's significance and omens—or dreamed that here at Lexington and Concord, on April 19, 1775, they themselves had been the instruments of destiny.

The long, eventful, turbulent day was over now and night had come, a night of stars and moon and whispering wind. The militiamen and minutemen turned wearily homeward. They were quiet, rather than jubilant. They did not foresee that stretching ahead for the cause they had served so valiantly were six years of ceaseless effort and sacrifice, of labor and hope and prayer, that from the arduous, grinding ordeal would emerge, finally and wonderfully, a new concept of human relations, a new experiment in government and a new nation, a democracy—the United States of America.

—And Afterward

The couriers bearing reports from Lexington and Concord reached New York in four days, Philadelphia in five days, Virginia in six, and the remote villages of the Carolinas in two weeks. It was evident then to all the colonists that their many years of bickering, argument and unheeded petitions to the King and Parliament had passed. They now were at war with England.

On May 10, 1775, the Second Continental Congress met in Philadelphia, and on June 15 appointed George Washington as commander-in-chief of the American forces. At Cambridge, July 3, Washington formally took command of these forces which comprised slightly more than 20,000 men and officers.

But already two other clashes between patriot and British soldiers had occurred.

On May 10, the same day that the Congress convened, Ethan Allen, the bluff and picturesque Vermont frontiersman, marched a band of his "Green Mountain Boys" to Ticonderoga and pounced upon the British fort there. According to Ethan Allen's own story of this incident, he called for, and obtained, the British colonel's surrender "in the name of the Great Jehovah and the Continental Congress." According to his Boys, Captain Allen had stalked into the fort and addressed the British colonel somewhat less ceremoniously—

by shouting, *"Come out, you damned old rat! Come out!"*

All through the month of May and the first weeks of June, General Gage's chastened regulars had been virtually bottled up in Boston, with companies of New England militia laying siege to the town. Gage had observed the rebels hovering around Breed's Hill and Bunker Hill, eminences that rose above Charlestown Neck. He was unpleasantly surprised, the morning of June 17, to discover them entrenched and fortified on Breed's Hill. Ordering an attack, he ferried five thousand redcoats to the bottom of the hill.

The bloody battle that ensued would be incorrectly known in history as the "Battle of Bunker Hill." Again and again the regulars climbed the steep incline to face a terrific fire from the Americans, a bombardment that stopped only when the Americans had exhausted their ammunition and were obliged to retreat. The encounter cost General Gage from one-third to one-half of his men, among them Major John Pitcairn. Soon afterward, the King angrily summoned Thomas Gage back to England and gave his post to a new commander, Sir William Howe. Included in the four hundred American losses at Breed's Hill was the splendid patriot, Dr. Joseph Warren.

The siege of Boston continued during the autumn and winter of 1775, and until March of 1776. Then Washington was able to take the offensive by seizing Dorchester Heights. With the Americans too close for comfort, Sir William Howe evacuated the town. In their transport ships, the British sailed, March 17, from the harbor to seek a better base for future operations.

Meanwhile, an American expedition into Canada had been disastrous. Advancing northward through the Maine forests, the Americans had hoped for military success and also to impress the Canadians and win them to the patriot cause. They found, instead, that the Canadians were cool to such overtures, and the American assault upon the city of Quebec on December 31, 1775, was a crippling defeat.

In selecting George Washington to head the colonial armies, the Congress had made a decision that would ultimately determine the result of the war. Besides absolute integrity and a peerless courage, Washington had unique vision. He could assess the patriot position, its strength as well as its weaknesses. He saw that his soldiers would be fighting on terrain familiar to them, and for a cherished principle, both favorable circumstances—but that they would always be inferior in numbers and resources to their adversaries. Though blessed with spirit, the colonies were materially poor, whereas the King was rich, the British regiments would have the bulwark of adequate provisions behind them. Sagacious and practical, Washington surmised that this struggle would not be brief. No, it might go on indefinitely, there might be intervals when the colonials lacked the proper implements for warfare, perhaps even the bare necessities of life.

They must be bound together, kept faithful through every stress and strain, and bravely Washington set himself to the enormous task. He was unquestionably the one man who could have accomplished it. That he somehow did so was the measure of his genius.

And yet, for all his wisdom, Washington would not have said in 1775 that the object of the war was to separate the colonies completely and forever from England. Those rebellious Americans who thought of independence as their true goal were still a mere handful, few and far between. The great majority wanted and were willing to fight for a rightful representation in their government and against the persecutions of a domineering monarch. Later, Washington was to admit candidly that in 1775 he had abhorred the idea of independence—and by midsummer of 1776, was convinced that nothing else would save the country. In 1776, Washington's viewpoint, like that of most patriots, underwent a profound change. There were several factors that brought about the change.

Now that the royal governors had been cast off, the legislative bodies of the various colonies were reorganizing, and in the process learning that they could capably choose new governors from among their own people, repeal old and detested laws, and enact new laws—an experience which was very reassuring. Also, Americans were reading and absorbing the widely circulated books, tracts and pamphlets of radical writers who boldly advocated the "common sense" of breaking away entirely from British rule. But even more, perhaps, public opinion was influenced at this time by King George's policy of employing professional soldiers to wage war in the colonies.

These soldiers were German mercenaries, in the service of German princes. They fought wherever their masters sent them. Eighteen thousand of them came from Hesse-Cassel to America in the summer of 1776; eventually there would be 30,000, mostly Hessians. The hiring of mercenaries was customary in Europe; to George III, himself a German prince, there seemed nothing peculiar about it. But the colonists thought of the Hessians as "paid murderers" and hated them. With the arrival of the first Hessian detachments, many Americans who had been hesitant before were eager to renounce any further allegiance to England and King George.

The Virginians were conspicuous in the movement toward independence. On June 7, Richard Henry Lee, chairman of the Virginia delegation to the Continental Congress, offered resolutions asserting "that these United Colonies are, and of right ought to be, free and independent states . . . that all political connection between them and the state of Great

Britain is, and ought to be, totally dissolved," and urging a confederation of the new states and the establishment of alliances with foreign powers. A committee composed of Thomas Jefferson, Benjamin Franklin, John Adams, Roger Sherman and Robert R. Livingston was appointed to draft a declaration of independence. When Lee's resolutions had been adopted, the declaration was written by Jefferson, with minor alterations by Franklin and Adams. On July 4, the momentous document was accepted by the Congress. Engrossed on parchment, it was signed August 2 by all but two members of Congress, whose signatures were added at a later date.

Thus, in 1776, the United States was created as a new nation in the world—though her military fortunes were just then at low ebb. The scene of the conflict had shifted. From Boston, Washington had gone directly to New York, thinking to defend that important seaport. But Sir William Howe had followed him with twice as many troops, available reinforcements and a British fleet in the harbor. In a series of losing battles, Washington was driven southward, across the Delaware River and into Pennsylvania. On Christmas night he managed to deliver a brilliant counter-stroke, recrossing the ice-choked Delaware and overwhelming Hessian regiments stationed at Trenton, New Jersey. At Princeton, January 3, he made another successful surprise attack, and afterward retired to winter quarters in Morristown.

The year of 1777 was to be the most fateful of the war. The British planned campaigns to capture Philadelphia and to isolate New England from the rest of the country by an invasion from Canada, down Lake Champlain and the Hudson River. The first campaign was quickly carried out despite Washington's valiant efforts to prevent it. Defeating the Americans at Brandywine Creek, Sir William Howe took possession of Philadelphia and the nearby forts, and won a sharp engagement at Germantown. But the invasion from the north, led by General John Burgoyne, was doomed to failure. The Americans had concentrated their strength, the militiamen had rallied to harass and delay Burgoyne. Sorely beset all along the way, the British were badly beaten in the Battle of Freeman's Farm in upstate New York. At Saratoga, October 17, Burgoyne surrendered his army of 5,700 men, their guns and equipment—a surrender that was to have resounding effects both in Europe and for America.

France had shrewdly eyed the combat between England and the colonies from the very start. The French and the English had been enemies for centuries. France still resented the drubbing England had administered upon her in the Seven Years' War, and she pined for revenge. Frenchmen felt that any blow that injured England was a blow for France. They had applauded the Declaration of Independence and recognized the existence of the United States as a nation. Occasionally and secretly the French government had contributed money and supplies to the Americans, with vague promises of more substantial assistance. But when, in 1776, Benjamin Franklin and other envoys of the United States had gone to Paris to attempt the negotiation of a treaty of alliance, France had been evasive, preferring to watch and wait. Now, believing that the Battle of Saratoga was a straw in the wind, the French officials received Franklin cordially. In February, 1778, France entered into two treaties with the Americans, one of alliance, one of commerce.

These treaties infuriated the English. Soon England and France were at war again in Europe, and England found herself fighting on two continents, oceans apart, a situation much to her disadvantage.

Though France's motives were calculating and business-like rather than generous, her aid to the United States was valuable and given at a time when it was desperately needed, for the months following the triumph at Saratoga were the darkest that the patriots had ever known. Washington was in winter quarters at Valley Forge, Pennsylvania; his troops were feeling the pinch of poverty, suffering every possible hardship. Their provisions were pitiably scanty, their weapons rapidly deteriorating, their clothing in rags, many of them were ill. Congress was strapped for funds and had not the means of raising funds by taxation.

Worst of all, perhaps, for the morale of civilians as well as soldiers, petty quarreling and jealousies had flared dangerously. Disgruntled army officers and suspicious members of Congress were conspiring to depose Washington as commander-in-chief and to replace him with General Horatio Gates. This intrigue was known as the Conway Cabal. When Washington met it with the fearlessness that he showed in every crisis, the plot was abandoned.

Throughout the war, Washington's popularity with his troops and with the American people was never in doubt. His military skill and the nobility of his character attracted to him such trained and talented European soldiers as the young and ardent Marquis de Lafayette from France, Count Casimir Pulaski and Thaddeus Kosciusko from Poland, Baron Johann De Kalb and Baron von Steuben from Germany, all of whom enlisted in his ranks and fought with great distinction for the patriot cause.

American spirits were stimulated in the spring of 1778 by bits of cheerful and welcome news. The youthful Virginian George Rogers Clark had led a western expedition, capturing forts at Cahokia, Kaskaskia and Vincennes, and sweeping the British from the area of the Ohio and Wabash rivers. Also, American sailors were conducting daring raids on British vessels. Indeed, Captain John Paul Jones had even ventured to cross the Atlantic into British waters, conquering English ships which he either destroyed or took as prizes. The American Navy had been hastily built; it was small, not one-twentieth the size of England's gigantic navy, a veritable midget by contrast. But its role in the Revolution was not insignificant. The Yankee seamen were a gallant lot, always giving a fine account of themselves.

On June 19, Washington marched out of his Valley Forge encampment with an army that had benefited by the milder weather, increased rations and additional stores purchased with money sent from France. The redcoats had evacuated Philadelphia, and Sir William Howe had been superseded in command by Sir Henry Clinton. Washington sturdily trailed Clinton into New Jersey, caught up with him at Monmouth Court House and attacked him, winning a battle that was heartening, though paid for with scores of American lives.

Relying on the strong Loyalist sentiment in the South to help him, Clinton then marched in that direction, captured Savannah, overran Georgia and re-established the royal government in the capital. The British next forged into South Carolina, seizing and occupying Charleston. American guerrilla bands in the region struck often, swiftly and unexpectedly at the invaders, but never quite halted them. Assuming that South Carolina was safely in British possession, Clinton turned back to New York, leaving Lord Cornwallis with 5,000 Loyalists and British regulars to hold it.

The years 1779 and 1780 were extremely difficult for Washington, made the more so by the shocking treason at West Point of Benedict Arnold, one of his most trusted officers and a cherished friend. With about half of the whole American force, Washington remained in the North, wary of tricks that Clinton might play. At Stony Point and at Paulus Hook, he briskly defeated Clinton's regiments and bagged a thousand prisoners. The winter of 1779–1780 he spent again at Morristown, sustaining and caring for his men, whose condition was nearly as depleted and critical as it had been at Valley Forge.

The spring of 1781 was a season of dreadful fighting in the South. General Nathanael Greene, leading an American army in the Carolinas, compelled the British to yield territory they had seized earlier; but in Virginia, Lord Cornwallis continued to raid and ravage the countryside mercilessly. At length, General Lafayette, Baron von Steuben and General Anthony Wayne combined their scattered troops, confronted Cornwallis and drove him to retreat.

In August, Cornwallis made his base at Yorktown, which he fortified. He was mapping a new campaign, and Yorktown, he thought, was a perfect spot for his purposes. Here he could rest a while. Here he could have access to Chesapeake Bay, and if he should desire reinforcements, Clinton could send them to him by sea from New York.

This was an error of judgment which Lord Cornwallis would bitterly mourn forever.

During the summer, several regiments of French infantrymen had arrived in New York to swell the numbers of the northern American army. Washington, too, was busy with plans, intending to make a full-scale assault on Clinton— when, suddenly, he learned that the French admiral, Comte de Grasse, had set sail August 13 for Chesapeake Bay, bringing a French fleet and three thousand more soldiers.

Washington saw at a glance what the information implied. If French ships were guarding the bay, Cornwallis could not get reinforcements from Clinton—from any quarter. No, the only chance of escape from his snug Yorktown haven would be by land. And an escape by land could be blocked!

Washington acted immediately. Organizing his troops, he moved southward at top speed, gathering in all the patriot companies in New Jersey and Virginia as he went. On September 29, he reached Yorktown—and there, as he had hoped, was de Grasse's fleet, anchored offshore. Deploying his ranks in a semicircle around the town, Washington advanced, snaring Cornwallis as neatly as a hunter might have treed a fox.

Cornwallis must have known from the first moment of the Americans' appearance on the horizon that the game was up, but for nineteen days he obstinately resisted their deliberate, relentless encroachment. Then, on October 17, bowing to the inevitable, he sent a white flag of truce to Washington, requesting a pause of twenty-four hours in which to arrange the terms of surrender.

The request was granted, the terms were arranged, and on October 19 the British laid down their arms.

With the fall of Yorktown, hostilities ceased in America. Deeply embroiled in the growing European war, where Spain had joined France against her, England was sick and tired of the struggle with her defiant colonies. How scheming they were, how incorrigible—and with what fantastic staying powers, bouncing back after reversals that should have crushed them!

Well, let them go! Good riddance, probably.

So the American Revolution ended abruptly and, for the patriots, in a blaze of glory. Though peace negotiations would not be completed for many months, the guns that had opened fire at Lexington and Concord on April 19, 1775, were hushed at last.

Now the United States could look beyond battlefields and bloodshed, forward to freedom.

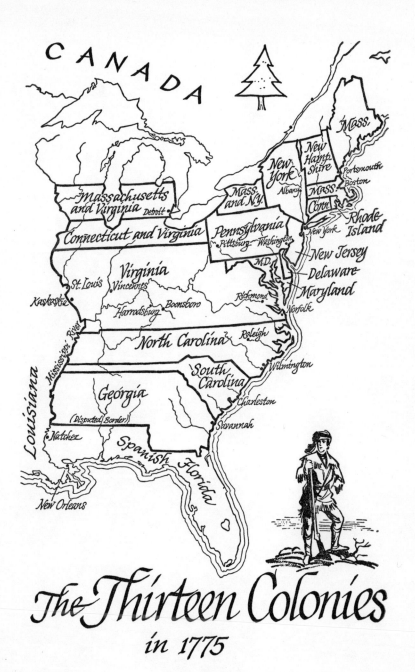

The Thirteen Colonies in 1775

Bibliography

ADAMS, James Truslow: *History of the United States.* New York, Charles Scribner's Sons, 1933.

ALLEN, Herbert S.: *John Hancock, Patriot in Purple.* New York, The Beechhurst Press, 1953.

BOWEN, Catherine Drinkwater: *John Adams and the American Revolution.* Boston, Little, Brown and Company, 1950.

CHANNING, Edward: *A Student's History of the United States.* New York, The Macmillan Company, 1911.

DORSON, Richard M.: *America Rebels, Narratives of the Patriots.* New York, Pantheon Books, Inc., 1953.

EATON, Jeanette: *That Lively Man, Benjamin Franklin.* New York, William Morrow and Company, 1948.

FAŸ, Bernard: *Franklin, the Apostle of Modern Times.* Boston, Little, Brown and Company, 1929.

FORBES, Esther: *Paul Revere and the World He Lived In.* Boston, Houghton Mifflin Company, 1942.

FRENCH, Allen: *The Day of Lexington and Concord.* Boston, Little, Brown and Company, 1925.

LOSSING, B. J.: *Pictorial Field Book of the Revolution.* New York, Harper and Brothers, 1850.

MONTROSE, Lynn: *Rag, Tag and Bobtail.* New York, Harper and Brothers, 1952.

PLUMB, J. H.: *The First Four Georges.* New York, The Macmillan Company, 1957.

SCHEER, George E., and RANKIN, Hugh F.: *Rebels and Redcoats.* Cleveland and New York, The World Publishing Company, 1957.

TOURTELLOT, Arthur Bernon: *William Diamond's Drum.* New York, Doubleday and Company, 1959.

WALLACE, Willard M.: *Appeal to Arms.* New York, Harper and Brothers, 1951.

WARD, Christopher: *The War of the Revolution.* New York, The Macmillan Company, 1952.

ALSO

American Heritage Book of the Revolution. New York, Simon and Schuster, 1958.

Autobiography of Benjamin Franklin, Edited by Frank Woodworth Pine. New York, Garden City Publishing Company, 1925.

Dictionary of American Biography. New York, Charles Scribner's Sons, 1936.

Encyclopaedia Britannica.

Encyclopedia of American History, Edited by Richard M. Morris. New York, Harper and Brothers, 1953.

Lexington and Concord, A Camera Impression. Samuel Chamberlain, New York, Hastings House, 1939.

Webster's Biographical Dictionary. Springfield, Massachusetts, G. C. Merriam Company, 1943.

Index

Adams, John, 60, 65, 71, 83-93, 121, 124-126, 176
Adams, Samuel, 59-61, 65-69, 72-74, 76, 79, 84-88, 94-96, 104-110, 111, 121; at First Continental Congress, 123-126, 132, 135, 137, 141-145, 149-152
Albany Plan, 44
Allen, Ethan, 172-173
American "patriots," 15, 18, 42; resentment of Stamp Act, 56-57; rallying at Concord, 155-160
American Revolution, 172-181
Arnold, Benedict, 179
Attucks, Crispus, 80-81
Auchmuty, Robert, 84, 85, 90
Augusta of Saxe-Gotha, 29-30

Barrett, Colonel John, 153-155, 157-160
Bentley, Joshua, 138-141
Bernard, Sir Francis, 57, 71, 81, 95
Boston, Massachusetts, 12, 14, 15-17, 45, 47, 56-60, 65-74; scene of Massacre, 78-82, 83-93; Boston Tea Party, 103-109; Port Bill, 112; port closed, 118; 173
Boston Common, 17, 46, 68, 71, 79, 95, 129, 135, 137
Bowdoin, James, 121
Braddock, General Edward, 37, 49-51, 119
British East India Company, the, 102-105, 111, 112, 118

Brown, John, minuteman killed at Lexington, 23
Brown, John, Rhode Island leader in Gaspee incident, 98-100
Brown, Reuben, 155, 160
Brown, Solomon, 143, 148
Brown, Thaddeus, 13
Buckman's Tavern, Lexington, 11, 13, 149-151
Bunker Hll, Battle of, 173
Burgoyne, General John, 177
Buttrick, Major John, 155-158, 160, 161

Cambridge, Massachusetts, 17, 123, 126, 127, 132, 137, 141, 148, 155, 167, 169, 172
Canada, French in, 32; English gains possessions, 33, 36, 113, 119, 122; failure of American campaign, 173-174; 176
Castle Island, 71, 87-88, 92, 107, 113, 115, 116
Charleston, South Carolina, 48, 103, 104, 114; captured by British, 179
Charlestown, Massachusetts, 123, 126, 127, 129, 137, 138, 141, 169, 173
Clark, General George Rogers, 178
Clark, Jonas, 132, 133, 143, 144, 149-150
Clark, Mrs. Jonas, 144, 145, 149
Clinton, Sir Henry, 178-180
Coercive Acts, 113

About the Author

Jeannette Covert Nolan was born in Indiana and has lived there all her life. Her forebears came to the Hoosier state as pioneers and her grandfather was one of its first editors. On graduation from high school she worked as a reporter and feature writer on newspapers in Evansville until she married. As her three children were growing up, she turned seriously to writing books, the first of which was published in 1932. Since then she has written many books of fiction and biography, also short stories, plays, and essays. She has taught creative writing at Indiana University and served as a staff member at five Writers' Conferences there; twice she conducted juvenile workshops at the University of Colorado Writers' Conference. Several of her books have been selected by the Junior Literary Guild.

In 1959 and again in 1961 she won the Indiana University Award for the "Most Distinguished Juvenile Book by an Indiana Author" published in those years.